Building Literacy Connections with Graphic Novels

Building Literacy Connections with Graphic Novels

Page by Page, Panel by Panel

Edited by

James Bucky Carter
University of Virginia

National Council of Teachers of English
1111 W. Kenyon Road, Urbana, Illinois 61801-1096

Staff Editor: Bonny Graham

Manuscript Editor: Susan Campanini

Interior Design: Doug Burnett

Cover Design: Pat Mayer

    The Scarlet Letter image: Pat Mayer

    Dragon and *The Wizard of Oz* images: ©2007 JupiterImages Corporation

NCTE Stock Number: 03920

It is the policy of NCTE in its journals and other publications to provide a fo-rum for the open discussion of ideas concerning the content and the teaching of English and the language arts. Publicity accorded to any particular point of view does not imply endorsement by the Executive Committee, the Board of Directors, or the membership at large, except in announcements of policy, where such endorsement is clearly specified.

Every effort has been made to provide current URLs and email addresses, but because of the rapidly changing nature of the Web, some sites and addresses may no longer be accessible.

Library of Congress Cataloging-in-Publication Data

Building literacy connections with graphic novels : page by page, panel by panel / edited by James Bucky Carter.
     p. cm.
  Includes bibliographical references.
  ISBN 978-0-8141-0392-0 (pbk.)
  1. Language arts. 2. Graphic novels—History and criticism. 3. Literacy. I. Carter, James Bucky, 1977–
LB1631.B773 2007
428.4'0712—dc22

                   2007002806

This book is dedicated to my mother, Gail, who bought me comics when she could and helped instill in me the value of hard work and doing well in school.

It is also dedicated to all of the teachers who have **tried,** *or at least* **wanted,** *to use comics and graphic novels in their classrooms and to all administrators and principals, with the gentle reminder to never say no to a great idea.*

Contents

Permission Acknowledgments

Foreword

Stephen Weiner
Maynard Public Library, Maynard, Massachusetts

As a high school senior in 1975, I taught a course on comic books to my peers. The teacher supervising my work found my choice of subject "daring," but, thirty years later, graphic novels, or "long comic books," have earned consideration for classroom use. Since comic books were introduced in the 1930s, creative publishers and teachers have sought ways to use them in the classroom. The 1940s saw superheroes such as Captain America and Superman delivering educational messages, and comic book series such as *The Classics Illustrated* attempted to bring literature to comic book readers. During the 1960s, some superheroes were imbued with greater characterization and cast in a Shakespearean tradition. In the late 1970s, the "graphic novel" was born—a story with a beginning, middle, and end, told in comic book form, that hoped to achieve the same emotional impact as a serious prose novel. Since the 1970s, the graphic novel form has grown by leaps and bounds, and now the term encompasses single narratives that treat serious subjects, as well as series of tales with ongoing characters such as the Amazing Spider-Man, and nonfiction accounts such as Joe Sacco's book on the Palestinian conflict in the Middle East.

Graphic novels are beginning to earn a natural place in the classroom because the comics format has grown to encompass many thought-provoking ideas as well as providing powerful storytelling. Art Spiegelman's *Maus*, the story of his parents' survival in World War II concentration camps, earned a special Pulitzer Prize, and many other graphic novels have won major awards, thus achieving literary status. Many graphic novels retell literary classics. Finally, some graphic novel series, such as Neil Gaiman's *Sandman*, are peopled with mythic and historic characters, making them natural springboards for reading the original literature. And because the history of American comics reflects the history of the United States itself, comics may be an effective way to bring history into classroom discussions.

Since *Maus* appeared in graphic novel form in 1986, a considerable number of literary graphic novels followed, constituting a "library" of books that could interest readers who were generally uninterested in comics, so much so that most major publishers are now bringing out their own graphic novels. In addition to adding something new to the curriculum, graphic novels are a good way to convey complex ideas. The comics format often makes information attractive and more easily digested. It is the world's most popular art form, and all types of readers naturally gravitate toward it. Anecdotes of the ways in which reading comics has attracted otherwise reluctant readers began appearing in the comics press as far back as 1968. The truth is that comics do in fact entice reluctant readers and struggling readers as well as good readers. We live at a time when the way in which information is presented changes continually. In the past, most information was presented in newspaper, magazine, or book format. Presently, information is delivered in a multitude of formats, such as the Internet and video, making it harder for readers to acquire the skills necessary to simply read a prose book because the text in these newer formats may not always be linear or narrative, or it may be less important than the surrounding visual elements. This makes using graphic novels especially important, because reading a graphic novel is closer to reading a traditional prose book or magazine than reading other visual media such as weblogs or instant messaging.

The book that you, the reader, are holding in your hands demonstrates why a growing number of today's educators feel that graphic novels and the classroom go together naturally. In a world where the young are always seeking the new, the comics format remains as fresh as the current pop hit and as useful as a Phillips head screw. I invite you to take the ideas proposed in this book into your classrooms and into your lives.

Acknowledgments

I would like to acknowledge the efforts of all of the contributors who helped make this collection possible by being so eager to share their excellent ideas and superb expertise; all of the publishers and artists who let us reprint their work; Dr. Joan Kaywell and everyone who initially helped me send out a "Call for Papers"; David Pugalee, for first letting me know it was "okay" to want to work with the topic of graphic novels in education; Dr. Joe Strzepek and Dr. Margo Figgins, for their continued support, which allowed me to grow my knowledge and vision; every single person reading the acknowledgments; and the wonderful folks at NCTE, especially Kurt Austin.

1 Introduction—Carving a Niche: Graphic Novels in the English Language Arts Classroom

James Bucky Carter
University of Virginia

There is a graphic novel for virtually every learner in your English language arts classroom. From students who "just like to look at pictures" to those who are prepared for a heady academic challenge, interests can be piqued and zones of proximal development (Vygotsky, 1978) enriched by reading a graphic novel, herein defined as a "book-length sequential art narrative featuring an anthology-style collection of comic art, a collection of reprinted comic book issues comprising a single story line (or arc), or an original, stand-alone graphic narrative" (Carter, 2004). Indeed, just as comics experienced a "Golden Age" of popularity in the United States in the 1940s, comics and the graphic novel are experiencing a burgeoning Golden Age in education today.

A substantial, expanding body of evidence asserts that using graphic novels and comics in the classroom produces effective learning opportunities over a wide range of subjects and benefits various student populations, from hesitant readers to gifted students. Studies of comics in the classroom go back to the 1940s at least, but, over the last decade, librarians have fervently led the way in making the case for graphic novels as exciting and proper reading material for adolescents. Many public libraries now have graphic novel sections or carry graphic novels in their stacks. Published studies by English language arts teachers who have used graphic novels in their classes have been relatively rare, however, and graphic novels still remain largely on the fringes of the profession.

But the marginalization of the graphic novel is changing rapidly. With the growing understanding of the importance of critical literacy, visual literacy, and other types of literacy that were once considered "alternate," more attention has been paid to graphic novels. The efforts of librarians have begun to pay off and to extend outside the domain of library conferences and publications. Books such as Michele Gorman's *Getting Graphic: Using Graphic Novels to Promote Literacy with Preteens and Teens* (2003) and Stephen Weiner's *101 Best Graphic Novels* (2001) and increased interest on behalf of NCTE journals and other education periodicals have brought graphic novels into the mainstream. A recent NCTE statement on multimodal literacies (2005) seems likely to encourage the growing presence of graphic novels in the classroom.

The media are helping to bring comics and graphic novels to the fore as well, with film adaptations of graphic novels such as *Ghost World*, *Road to Perdition*, *From Hell*, and *American Splendor*, which are consistently raking in major returns for moviemakers. The popularity of these films shows that there is much more to these books than superheroes in leotards and capes. At the same time, movies based on superheroes also remain popular, helping to engage a new generation of young fans. This engagement might help teachers to accept the presence of a comic in class. Likewise, the efforts of classroom teachers and university-level educators have drawn the attention of mainstream media. For example, National Public Radio's broadcast of *Morning Edition* on April 8, 2005, and a broadcast of CBS's *The Early Show* on March 25, 2005, both featured stories about a Maryland school district's acceptance and promotion of comics in the classroom (Hughes, 2005) as a means to get otherwise disinclined or struggling students motivated about reading. *The Christian Science Monitor* has picked up on the trend as well (see "'Hamlet' Too Hard? Try a Comic Book" in the issue of October 12, 2004). On March 3 of the same year, *USA Today* published an article entitled "Teachers Are Getting Graphic" (Toppo, 2005). This is but a sampling of the many articles that have appeared in the past few years.

Students are doing their part to promote graphic novels as well. Manga, the Japanese equivalent of the graphic novel, is amazingly popular with students (Wilson, 1999). In 2003, when I noticed one of my sixth graders reading a manga, I polled the class. Seventy-five percent of them had read and enjoyed a manga recently and 80 percent knew what a manga was. Informal as they are, those numbers included female students, who flock to manga (Bucher & Manning, 2004; Reid, 2002), and they were taken at a middle school that is not in New York or Los Angeles, but in a tiny town in rural North Carolina. Manga are so popular now, as are graphic novels, that major book chains such as Barnes and Noble give them their own sections.

Of course, to persuade most English language arts teachers, and perhaps you, the reader, to consider graphic novels as serious resources for the classroom, more convincing evidence is in order than what might be dismissed as a fad or passing spike in a medium's popularity. Research and applied examples would help, wouldn't they? The chapters that follow offer practical ideas and applications from experienced teachers, professors, and education professionals for using graphic novels in conjunction with printed texts you might already be exploring with your students. Many of the contributors presently teach graphic novels in their classes or have previously done so, and they see young people at various levels enthralled in these diverse examples of sequential art narratives. Before reading their fine essays, however, consider this introduction as a glimpse into some of the most salient current research on the utility of comics and graphic novels in education.

An Arts-Rich Education

Recent studies detailing the benefits of an arts-rich education suggest that teachers of English language arts might want to reexamine how they incorporate the arts into their pedagogy. The idea is to remember what John Dewey (1916) said:

> Not only is social life identical with communication, but all communication (and hence all genuine social life) is educative. To be a recipient of a communication is to have an enlarged and changed experience. . . . The experience has to be formulated in order to be communicated. The formulate requires getting outside of it, seeing it as another would see it, considering what points of contact it has with the life of another so that it may be got into such form that he can appreciate its meaning. . . . All communication is like art . . . (http://www.ilt.columbia.edu/publications/dewey.html)

In other words, a good education—one bound in experience and meaning making—is probably an education that has been enriched with a broad definition of art and culture.

Supporting such a claim is the 1999 report *Champions of Change: The Impact of the Arts on Learning*, which found through multiple extensive studies that "learners can attain higher levels of achievement through their engagement with the arts. Moreover . . . learning in and through the arts can help 'level the playing field' for youngsters from disadvantaged circumstances" (Fiske, p. viii). In an era in which closing the gap is of deep import, the study's finding that "high arts participation makes a more significant difference to students from low-income backgrounds than for high-income students" (p. viii) should raise eyebrows.

Champions of Change notes that the arts alter learning experiences in the following ways:

- The arts reach students who are not otherwise being reached.
- The arts reach students in ways that they are not otherwise being reached.
- The arts connect students to themselves and each other.
- The arts transform the environment for learning.
- The arts provide learning opportunities for adults in the lives of young people.
- The arts provide new challenges for those students already considered successful.
- The arts connect learning experiences to the world of real work. (pp. ix–x)

Especially in terms of project-based learning, the study demonstrates clearly that arts enhance learning (pp. x–xii). In terms of policy, the report summary concludes, "We must look to the arts as a vehicle for preparing entrants to the teaching profession" (p. xi); in other words, all teachers need to pay closer attention to the arts. The study shows strong connections among the arts and retention, self-image, and academic progress.

Critical Links: Learning in the Arts and Student Academic and Social Development (Deasy, 2002) explores the connections between the arts and literacy and language development. For example, researchers found "that visual art provide[d] a concrete 'metacognitive marking point'" for two male, learning disabled, reluctant readers and may help those already interested in visual arts to be more motivated to read (p. 144). Researchers asking the question "Is teaching reading through art more effective than teaching reading alone?" conclude that their meta-analysis "revealed a positive, moderately sized relationship between reading improvement and an integrated arts-reading form of instruction," although they admit that their sample size was limited (p. 138). Multiple studies in *Critical Links* show that "visual and performing arts can advance students' oral and written verbal forms" and that "the arts and oral and written language share interrelated physical and symbolic processes" (Deasy, 2004, p. 10).

The Comic Book Project and Dual Coding

The Comic Book Project, an after-school partnership between Michael Bitz, Teachers College at Columbia University, and Dark Horse Comics, Inc., illustrates the role of sequential art in enriching educational experiences. Whereas others have successfully shown the appeal and interest to younger students of comics during the school day (Dyson, 1997), Bitz worked with older students as well and in after-school sites. The project was designed "as a way of putting into practice some of the most important educational research of the last decade—that is, the correlation between involvement in the arts and performance in academic subjects," namely, the Fiske and Deasy studies (Bitz, 2004, p.33). Bitz also drew from other studies demonstrating "that children discover meaningful dimensions of their worlds when they can explore them through creative arts, including comic books" (Bitz, p. 575). In the fall of 2002, "733 children at 33 after-school sites in New York city brainstormed, outlined, sketched, wrote, and designed original comic books" (p. 574). The goal was "to build literacy and artistic skills while motivating children not only to attend the sessions but also to take ownership of and pride in their work" (p. 575). Guided by specially trained instructors, students from grades 4–8 (Bitz now has worked with high schoolers as well) used professionally created templates to create sequential narratives in which words and images were in every panel (p. 577) and engaged in workshop activities designed for sharing and critiquing with the aim of completing and "publishing" their own eight-page comics (p. 578–79). Bitz reports that, although many students were familiar with the superhero theme in comics, most of their own personal sequential narratives "were based on the hard reality of living in an inner-city environment" (p. 580). Based on surveys distributed to instructors and students, Bitz also found the following:

- Eighty-six percent of students felt the project helped them improve their writing.
- Ninety-two percent said they liked their own stories as a result of the project.
- Eighty-eight percent said they look to pictures for clues in stories because of the project.
- Ninety percent of instructors felt that their students' writing was improving.
- Ninety percent of instructors felt that, as a result of the project, their students like to write their own stories. (p. 582).

Open-ended questions solicited comments such as "This was the first time I got my kids to write without complaining about it" and "Living in the city, these children see a lot of things that aren't so positive. A project like this gives them the chance to express what's happening around them" (p. 582). Although students weren't informed of them, the goals of the project aligned with New York State's Learning Standards for English Language Arts, and Bitz's publications explore how each standard was met (p. 584). In examining implications for teachers, Bitz explains:

> Many of the manuscripts highlighted how students corrected and revised their own work, or demonstrated opportunities for instructors to show students where mistakes were made on a small scale (grammar and mechanics) or a large scale (story structure and thematic consistency). Also, one can observe noticeable improvement in writing from the manuscripts to the final comic books—mechanical errors were fixed, story structures were tightened, and character voices were honed. . . . The Comic Book Project seemed to have most marked effect on children with limited English proficiency. . . . According to instructors, these children's manuscripts and comic books represent more writing than they had produced in English class throughout the entire school year. (p. 585)

It is of interest to note that, whereas comic books are most known either for superpowered individuals wearing tights and fighting other equally powered and similarly attired foes or for the goofy and humorous characters who led to the genre's name (first "funnies," then "comics"), many students in The Comic Book Project created works in formats more advanced and more readily recognized as valuable in the English language arts community: authentic texts and autobiographical sketches. Indeed, in this regard, their comics are actually more like graphic novels (with many sterling examples of the form being autobiographical) than comic books.

In addition, English language learners' (ELL) interaction with comics has recently received attention in the *TESOL Quarterly*. Jun Liu reports that low-level students who received a high-level text with a comic strip "scored significantly higher than the low-level students receiving the high-level text only" (2004, p. 235). Although the comic strips that Liu's students used did not help comprehension in all cases, this outcome is still impressive and echoes Bitz's findings that comics can aid ELL populations in certain circumstances. Also worth noting in the Liu study is the talk of dual coding studies by the likes of Gambrell and Jawitz (1993) and Mayer (1999), who "found that words and pictures together produced better recall and transfer than either did alone, and that individual differences in ability were a factor" (Liu, 2004, p. 228). Dual coding is emerging as a theory that will no doubt provide even more evidence for teachers of English language arts to integrate more sequential art into their classrooms.

With research showing the importance of the arts in so many facets of student development and the interdependency of word and image in the graphic novel, it seems a natural progression for text-trusting English language arts teachers to gravitate toward visual arts to help them ease into more arts-intensive modes of teaching and learning. This book is one attempt to help teachers integrate the visual arts into the curriculum. Graphic novels, after all, are the perfect blend of word and picture, story as text and story as art. As such, they offer important, unique, and timely multiliteracy experiences.

Graphic Novels and Literacy

The bulk of current advocacy for the graphic novel has tried to tie the medium not so much to the beneficial elements of an arts-rich environment, as made clear in the Fiske and Deasy studies (Bitz, 2004), but more directly to notions of models of literacy, elements of pedagogy that teachers of English language arts are more comfortable exploring and, certainly, with which they are more engaged in their everyday teaching. This is a somewhat ironic trend, considering the work of educators with strong "English teacher cross-over appeal" such as Maxine Greene (1995), John Goodlad (2004), Henry Giroux (1992), and Eliot Eisner (1998). These scholars basically continue to say what Dewey seemed to hint at so many years ago: artistic experiences are important in developing literacy and critical thinking skills. This is also a major point of the Fiske and Deasy studies, which may not be familiar to many English language arts teachers. The present collection of essays by teachers overtly applies this line of thinking as well.

To understand thoroughly the promise of the graphic novel as an aid to more conventional notions of literacy, it is important to review what the notion of literacy signifies in contemporary educational talk and practice.

Karen Cadiero-Kaplan (2002) provides an excellent basic summary of literacy research and theories in her article "Literacy Ideologies: Critically Engaging the Language Arts Curriculum." She explains that there are at least four definitive literacies at work in today's classrooms:

- *functional literacy*, defined as having the skills "to be a productive citizen or member of the workforce" (p. 374)

- *cultural literacy*, the idea that there are certain things that everyone should know to be considered educated, competent citizens (e.g., E. D. Hirsch)

- *progressive literacy*, a constructivist approach to creating highly individualistic notions of what learning and living entail

- *critical literacy*, a postmodern (Meacham & Buendia, 1999), radical notion that can be defined as "a literacy of social transformation in which the ideological foundations of knowledge, culture, schooling, and identity-making are recognized as unavoidably political" and in which students engage critically in reading "the world and the word, by using dialogue to engage texts and discourses inside and outside the classroom" (p. 377).

Critical literacy is favored by Cadiero-Kaplan herself and is prominent in the work of Stanley Aronowitz, Henry Giroux and, most notably, Paulo Freire.

Gretchen E. Schwarz tackles this graphic novel-literacy connection directly in her article "Graphic Novels for Multiple Literacies" (2002). Hearkening to the ideals of critical and visual literacy, she explains that "in an increasingly visual culture, literacy educators can profit from the use of graphic novels in the classroom, especially for young adults" (2002, p. 1). Not only do graphic novels promote literacy (Lavin, 1998; Weiner, 2002), but they "offer value, variety, and a new medium for literacy that acknowledges the impact of visuals" (p. 1). Furthermore, Schwarz asserts that "An important benefit of graphic novels is that they present alternative views of culture, history and human life in general in accessible ways" (p. 3), tying the graphic novel to progressive, cultural, and critical notions of literacy. With respect to functional literacy, Schwarz suggests that graphic novels can be used for teaching literary terms and techniques and that social studies is a curricular area in which they are particularly strong and can easily be used across-the-curriculum: "graphic novels can bring new life beyond bland textbooks" (p. 2). Indeed, many graphic novels that are considered at the top of their format deal with political and social issues.

Although Schwarz (2002) gives no concrete examples (the present collection of essays seeks to remedy this problem), she explains that she is aware of some English teachers who make use of graphic novels in their classes and further persuades her readership of their worth by citing graphic novels developed specifically for aiding academics, such as "*McLuhan for Beginners* (Gordon & Willmarth, 1997) and *Introducing Cultural Studies* (Sardar & Van Loon, 1998)" (p. 2). Indeed, National Public Radio has recently brought the graphic novel *Dignifying Science* back into the national spotlight by featuring a broadcast on the work's excellent educational value and special role in getting female students interested in the sciences (the book details the contributions of women scientists around the world).

Timothy Morrison, Gregory Bryan, and George Chilcoat corroborate much of what Schwarz asserts in their article "Using Student-Generated Comic Books in the Classroom" (2002). They believe that "popular culture is integral to the lives of most middle school students. Use of popular culture can, therefore, diminish the disparity children perceive between their lives in and out of school by legitimizing their after school pursuits" (p. 738; Buckingham, 1998). This line of thinking, of course, fits well into progressive and cultural literacy theories. The authors suggest that teachers tap into this aspect of comics and graphic novels by having students create their own comic books:

> It is evident that comics are familiar to and popular with middle and high school students. The comic is a form of literature these students enjoy. Given the opportunity to create and share their own comic books, students engage in greater literacy exploration than they otherwise would, due to comics' popular and easily accessible format. (p. 759)

Again, the tie to the constructivism of progressive literacy is obvious. The authors conclude by mentioning the students' enthusiasm for the projects and providing a reminder that such activities engage in cross-curricular pursuits by embracing "language arts, visual arts, and content areas" (p. 767).

Education Week has continued the trend of exploring graphic novels as a means of engaging reluctant readers (Ingram, 2003; Galley, 2004). Stephen Cary has published *Going Graphic: Comics at Work in the Multilingual Classroom* (2004) as further evidence of the medium's effects on TESL/TEFL populations. *English Journal* is coming around to graphic novels and giving some much needed serious attention to their use by practicing teachers. Nancy Frey and Douglas Fisher shared their success in using graphic novels as scaffolding devices in their teaching of high school writing (January 2004, p. 19). Indeed, their article "Using Graphic Novels, Anime, and the Internet in an Urban High School" won NCTE's Farmer Award for Outstanding Writing. We are fortunate to reprint that essay herein and to have them contributing a new essay as well that gives teachers a great structural guide to using graphic novels in a fully textually integrated English language arts classroom. Jodi Leckbee wrote in *English Journal* that graphic novels are great for helping students transcend their apathy for reading (May 2004, p. 21) in response to the posed question "What activity has been most effective in assisting high school students to read?" More recently (November 2004, pp. 114–18), editor Don Gallo asked librarian Stephen Weiner to formally introduce graphic novels to *English Journal*'s readers in the Bold Books for Innovating Teaching section, and *The Council Chronicle* for September 2005 features two articles on graphic novels and comics. *NEAToday* even got in on the action in February 2005, with Thomas Grillo's article "Back to the Future: How Teachers Are Using Old Favorites to Hook the Newest Generations of Reluctant Adolescent Readers." What's the hook? Comic books, of course.

The hook of comics can be especially strong for boys. In their longitudinal study of male reading habits (*Reading Don't Fix No Chevys*, 2002), Michael W. Smith and Jeffrey D. Wilhelm found that graphic novels are one of the few types of texts that consistently engage male readers. Edgy, engaging, and different (pp. 148–57), graphic novels satisfied boys' overwhelmingly clear urge to explore visual texts. The authors state, "The intense importance of the visual as they engaged with all forms of texts was evident" and " a few engaged readers in this study all described their reading of books and stories in strikingly visual terms" (pp. 151–52). Important to our work in this collection of essays is their assertion that "A challenge here is for teachers to develop ways to assist boys who do not visualize what they read to develop ways of doing so. Otherwise they will not experience the same engagement with written texts that they do with multimedia ones" (p. 152). Graphic novels and comics, mostly produced for and consumed by males, give knowledgeable teachers a means to help show boys that, not only successful readers, but also successful writers and artists visualize as they work. (For other books with testimonials about comics from students and teachers, try Krashen's *The Power of Reading* [2002] and Shelley Hong Xu's *Trading Cards to Comic Strips* [2005].)

Among recent graphic novel proponents, Michele Gorman, a librarian from Austin, Texas, has done much for the format's new positioning in education via her book *Getting Graphic: Using Graphic Novels to Promote Literacy with Preteens and Teens* (2003). She asserts, "Research done by professionals in the field and real-life experience of librarians have shown that there is one format that covers a variety of genres, addresses current and relative issues for teens, stimulates the young people's imagination, and engages reluctant readers: graphic novels" (2003, p. xi). Gorman joins a rather extensive list of librarians who have been carrying the torch for graphic novels as aids to literacy (DeCandido, 1990; Bruggeman, 1997; Lavin, 1998; Weiner, 2002; Goldsmith, 2003) in their own professional journals and conferences. Indeed, the American

Library Association's Young Adult Library Services Association presented the theme "Getting Graphic @ Your Library" for Teen Read Week 2002 (Gorman, 2003).

Gorman's text is a teacher-friendly, workbook-like product that features a history of the format, how-to guides for ordering and teaching graphic novels, and activities for teachers and libraries interested in integrating the format into their classes. More important, she offers persuasive facts and down-to-earth ethos to tempt reluctant teachers and librarians into adding the books to their schools' shelves:

- Larry Dorrell and Ed Carol noted an 82 percent increase in library circulation when comics were added to a junior high library (Gorman, 2003, p. xi).
- The current generation "is more comfortable with non-text visual media" = "at ease" with combining words and pictures (p. 9).
- Graphic novels may act as intermediaries from the computer or television to print media (p. 9).
- Graphic novels engage reluctant readers (p. 9).
- Stephen Krashen (1996) has supplied research that the format is beneficial to ELL readers (p. 11).
- Visual messages alongside minimal print help ease frustrations of beginning or struggling readers (p. 11).

Accompanying these facts are charts detailing connections of various graphic novels to literary devices, a section on curriculum integration, and a suggested reading list, complete with accurate "grading" of titles (e.g., M = mature). The book is highly recommended for individual teachers and for schools' professional development libraries, along with Stephen Weiner's *The 101 Best Graphic Novels* (2001).

More on Graphic Novels and Visual Literacy

There are those scholars and researchers in various fields who promote visual literacy as its own distinctive skill. Like the graphic novel, visual literacy is gaining more ground as a viable entity of study and practice in public schools. The International Visual Literacy Association defines visual literacy as

> a group of vision competencies a human being can develop by seeing and at the same time having and integrating other sensory experiences. The development of these competencies is fundamental to normal human learning. When developed, they enable a visually literate person to discriminate and interpret the

> visual actions, objects, and/or symbols, natural or man-made,
> that are [encountered] in [the] environment. Through the creative
> use of these competencies, [we are] able to communicate with
> others. Through the appreciative use of these competencies, [we
> are] able to comprehend and enjoy the masterworks of visual
> communications (Fransecky & Debes, 1972, p. 7). (http://www.
> ivla.org/, 2003)

Mostly, visual literacy has been tied to the fields of graphic design, art,
and art history, but, over the last few decades, visual literacy, cultural
literacy, and critical literacy have become more and more intertwined.
Consider NCTE's recent statement on multimodal literacies (http://
www.ncte.org/about/over/positions/category/media/123213.htm),
which makes it clear that English teachers can no longer disregard the
visual. Miles Myers foretold this in 1996:

> English studies should include translations from one sign sys-
> tem to another as an essential part of the curriculum. These should
> include translating words into action—"acting out" scenes from
> stories, poems, and dramas—and novels to films, reports to
> speeches, paintings to descriptions. This means that students in
> English need to begin to give substantially more attention to vari-
> ous media. (p. 191)

Now we must heed his words more than ever (see Peggy Albers's
"Imagining the Possibilities in Multimodal Curriculum Design" in *English Education* [January 2006] for an explication of this Myers quote and
more discussion of multimodalities).

The contemporary view of literacy, then, is changing such that
texts are no longer considered simply words on a page, but anything in
the surrounding world of the literate person. And the literate person is
one who can "read" these various texts, whether written or visual, one
who can read the word and the world (Freire & Macedo, 1987).

Sequential art scholars Scott McCloud (1999), Chris Murray
(1997), and Neil Cohn (2003) have explored visual literacy in relation
to comics and graphic novels. Cohn espouses a theory of visual language
that echoes the underpinnings of critical and visual literacy. By examining sequence images, such as those seen in the panel breakdowns of
comics and graphic novels, Cohn believes one can see a "dynamic and
hierarchical thought process—just like in language" (www.emaki.net,
2003). Essentially, he says that "'images in sequence' are actually a language . . . the same as words in sequence." Obviously, the graphic novel
can offer a rich and stimulating means by which to develop the visual
literacy of students. As more research on dual coding develops, sequen-

tial art seems destined to have an even more prominent place in the English language arts classroom.

Lead-in to Case Study

Graphic novels are clearly gaining ground in public middle and high schools. However, texts such as Gorman's are very recent. If students are to gain the full literacy benefits of the format, we need many more practical articles that describe educational experiments and classroom success stories from middle and high school teachers who have used graphic novels. Most articles on graphic novels and the classroom, whether research or applied practice in orientation, come from college professors. Indeed, at the college level, the graphic novel enjoys more of the respect it deserves. What is needed is more evidence from researchers that graphic novels improve literacy skills. These research studies would necessarily be conducted in concert with evidence from teachers who have used the format successfully, but these articles are also still relatively scarce. Although it is hoped that teachers might be convinced by this collection of essays and similar works to try comics or graphic novels in the classroom, more needs to be written to be sufficiently compelling for the most conservative educators.

The section that follows is a further attempt at driving home the practical side of teaching comics or graphic novels in higher education, in summer programs, and, specifically, in North Carolina's public school system. I present a personal case study of my own successes using the format to illustrate how comics or graphic novels can be used to help reluctant or struggling readers as well as gifted readers. My efforts to teach Spiegelman's *Maus* (1986; 1991) to an academically and intellectually gifted eighth-grade classroom are chronicled as a means of documenting the struggles the graphic form still must overcome to gain acceptance. I also explore other activities using sequential art narratives that my students and I enjoyed.

A Personal Case Study

I could provide you with numerous research articles, but, if you are like most practicing middle and high school teachers I know, nothing persuades you like real-life, down-to-earth experiences. That is another reason why the essays in this collection are so valuable: they represent the ideas and, often, the actual hands-on attempts of experienced, respected teachers in various levels of education. But let me take an editor's prerogative for a moment and go even further. Allow me, if you will, to tell you the role that comic books and graphic novels have played in my own development as a child, as an adult, and as a teacher.

I have been reading comics since I could read anything. My teenage mother read them to me before I was literate because, I imagine, they were cheap and we were poor and because, as a high school dropout, she was probably sick of the more traditional texts she once confronted in school. To this day most of her own reading consists of the chance novel, the Bible, and an occasional magazine, although she has rediscovered joy in the act of reading, and her efforts with comics certainly helped instill in me a love and appreciation of art and literature that has yielded degrees in both disciplines and a strong desire to see them shared with everyone. My first teaching job, in 1999, was at a high school in a suburb of Charlotte, North Carolina, and my toughest assignment was to take a group of remedial readers in a grades 9–12 combination class and mold them into at least partially motivated literates capable of enjoying written work—and passing North Carolina's "gateway" reading test, which they had taken unsuccessfully for the first time in grade 8. The class was a snapshot of typically difficult-to-teach students: 504 plans, IEPs, poverty, drug and gang issues, family and personal traumas (including homelessness and stabbings) made up their day-to-day existence.

Since I was short on supplies to begin with, I was eager to augment my curriculum, and I turned to comics for help. After getting a local vendor to donate more than $200 worth of comics, I began to incorporate them into our everyday lessons. For example, when we read Rodman Philbrick's *Freak the Mighty*, I first used comics as complements to the classics, reinforcing the difficult concept of symbiotic relationships and interdependency by pairing the text with a Spider-Man comic in which Spidey fights Venom and Carnage, two alien villains who bond to human hosts, thereby creating symbiotic relationships. The contrast is, of course, that Philbrick's characters share a fairly healthy interdependency, whereas poor Peter Parker experiences the direct badness that symbiotic or co-dependent relationships can entail (see Figure 1.1).

The classroom conversations on good and bad relationships were poignant, in no small part due to the students' ability to connect to the themes and because of the immediate connection to popular culture via comics (remember Morrison, Bryan, & Chilcoat, 2002).

I integrated comics again later in the semester as it became more apparent to me that a lack of role models and a poor sense of connection to the school also plagued my students. The school's mascot was

Figure 1.1. Spider-Man asks Freak and Max if they want to exchange burdens.

an ambiguous abstraction called simply the "Wonder," and the lack of a readily identifiable mascot to accompany the odd name troubled me since I know students take pleasure and comfort in having a school identity. I created an African American superhero clad in the school's colors and whose nemesis was named after the school's rival institution (see Figure 1.2), and I used these icons to help engage my students in creative writing and in gaining an understanding of the concept of characterization.

We watched the superhero spoof film *Mystery Men* and noted the elements of superheroes, an easy enough task since the movie pokes fun at superhero clichés. We then applied our learning to create a group vision of our school hero's origin, powers, gadgets, and adventures. We examined heroes again as we awaited the arrival of Alice Childress's novel *A Hero Ain't Nothin' but a Sandwich*. I created template drawings

Figure 1.2. A new Wonder superhero mascot.

of a male and female superhero body and asked them to create their
own heroes with individual origins, powers, nemeses, love interests, etc.
Similar templates can be found in Gorman's text (2003, pp. 42–43). Dis-
appointment and a little shock ensued as two students created heroes
with marijuana-inspired powers, but overall, the group engaged well
in literary devices (e.g., origin, nemesis), genre studies, and general discussion about "what makes a hero." Students enjoyed the activity and
learned several complex concepts that had previously escaped their
grasp.

    While earning my MA in English at the University of Tennessee,
I taught a weeklong course on creative writing and another involving
sequential art (a create-your-own-comic-book course) to students rang-
ing from elementary to high school as part of the Kids U summer pro-

gram. Some of the parents remarked that their children had come alive for the first time doing their homework, which was reminiscent of comments from the Bitz studies (2004). Although some students still struggled, those who dug into the course did so with real fervor.

Also while I was at UT, I taught in my English 102 class Alan Moore and Dave Gibbons's graphic novel *Watchmen* (1987) as a text representative of late twentieth-century nuclear hysteria fiction and as a prophecy text due to its eerie similarities to 9/11 (massive destruction of Manhattan; a villain who was once supported by the United States and can even be considered a freedom fighter rather than evildoer, depending on one's point of view; the concept of war and horrific events bringing unity). The discussion yielded much evidence that students could engage in critical discourse wrapped around a graphic novel as the central text. This *augmentative* take in conventional curriculum (according to which the graphic novel increases the number of primary texts from which teachers can draw) is one that I hope middle and high school teachers will eventually use with sequential art narratives, as opposed to the more common *supplemental* take (where comics or graphic novels act as secondary extras to more accepted or canonical texts). But I understand—we must start somewhere. Most of the essays in this collection feature graphic novels paired with more traditional texts. It is true that graphic novels can be bridges (Farrell, 1966) to traditional texts. The opposite is true as well, but often what surfaces in the essays is the notion of a variety of texts working together as equal partners.

After finishing my studies at UT, I returned to teaching, as the academically and intellectually gifted specialist at a middle school in rural North Carolina. Once again, I used comics in my curriculum. Just as research indicates that comics and graphic novels can help ELL and literacy-challenged populations, it has also suggested that they can have a positive effect on the lives and learning of gifted students. Mitchell and George (1996), for example, suggest that comics fit well with teaching gifted children about morals and ethics.

In my grade 6 language arts class, I used comics to help students explore formats that are typically outside the realm of genre studies taught in regular classrooms. Furthermore, when other teachers approached me about lack of detail in their students' writing, Spidey and I again teamed up. I taught a personally crafted lesson entitled "The Comic Book Show 'n' Tell," an activity described in more detail in Chapter 10.

However, when I decided to take the leap from using simple, single-issue comics in my lessons to including a complex graphic novel,

I ran into trouble, clearly illustrating the existence of problems that the still-budding format has to overcome to stake a place in education. These are challenging problems that teachers, especially young teachers, who are perhaps those most willing and eager to accept graphic novels as serious texts and worthy classroom resources, must be ready to face.

My attempts to teach *Maus I* and *II* (Spiegelman,1986; 1991) to an academically and intellectually gifted grade 8 language arts class were stifled when a county administrator decided that the books were inappropriate for middle schoolers, (I have since learned of a central Virginia teacher who uses *Maus* in her grade 6 public school class and of many other schools nationwide, both public and private, that use the text.) I was shocked by the administrator's decision. To write a rationale for using these books had never crossed my mind; that was a mistake I made that young teachers reading this could learn from. In my head, *Maus* was such an exemplary text that anyone would have gladly welcomed it in the classroom. For those of you who might want to know what specifically was considered inappropriate, I will tell you what I didn't know to look out for and you can make up your own minds (or discuss it with colleagues) as to whether your community standards would be in conflict with the contents. The culprit was on page 30 of *Maus I* (see Figure 1.3). On this page, the elderly Vladek, Art's father, tells how Art's arm had to be broken for him to be born and how, for a few years, the young Art's arm would pop up. "We joked and called you 'Heil Hitler!'" says Vladek (Spiegelman, 1986).

In his gesticulations, Vladek knocks over his medication and begins to re-count his daily pills. To me, this is one of the most powerful pages in the book, a point where it is apparent that a man who was strong enough to survive the Holocaust is now at the mercy of his own aging body.

Two months after I missed my chance to teach *Maus*, Gorman placed the book (which she does rate as "M" for "mature") on her list of "10 'Safe' Graphic Novels for Even the Most Conservative Libraries" (2003, p. 71), stating, "In spite of the harsh themes, this Pulitzer Prize Award-winning graphic novel is a classic and has a place on library shelves for its literary merit and historical importance" (p. 71). Furthermore, the same text and images that were found unsuitable by my school administrator were recently reprinted in *The New Smithsonian Book of Comic-Book Stories* (Callahan, 2004). I hope this illustrates vividly that I know firsthand how difficult it can be to encourage others to approve some of the ideas offered in this collection. My hope is that, once this book helps you become confident in using the vast educational poten-

Figure 1.3. A panel from Spiegelman's *Maus I* was deemed objectionable by one school administrator.

tial of graphic novels, you will also let it help you win administrative battles that I didn't even see coming.

Later that same school year, I led my sixth graders in creating "how-to" comic books (for example, "how to bake cookies," "how to wash a car") and biographical sequential narratives based on historical figures that were important to them (e.g., The Wright Brothers, Clay Aiken, Kenny Chesney). I couldn't teach the particular graphic novel I had wanted to share with my students, but I would teach my students to produce and publish (for the other grade 6 classes, anyway) their own comic!

Climbing the Hill: Others' Problems with Graphic Novels

This example of "cat and *Maus*" perfectly illustrates the hill that proponents of the graphic novel are still climbing in many areas. Perhaps it is the relative newness of the format or the mature themes addressed by most graphic novels that some teachers and administrators find so unsettling. Who knows? Maybe there is still fallout from Frederic Wertham's infamous 1954 text (now widely debunked), *Seduction of the Innocent*, in which the McCarthy-era doctor explains that comics contribute to social decay by supporting violence and homosexuality. But this seems a stretch. Although plenty of the horror and crime comics on the market in the 1950s would still give conservative parents cause for alarm, Wertham focused too much on the superhero genre, which, at the time, was far from morose or delinquent. Perhaps it is the word-picture association itself that is disturbing. Maybe teachers feel that comics are too "childish" for students (Marsh & Millard, 2000; Weiner, 2004), regardless of evidence to the contrary. The basis of teachers' cautions about accepting graphic novels as classroom material is another area where much research is needed. Until we understand the problem, we cannot ask teachers to accept our solutions. But we can give them as large and practical an arsenal of resources as possible. That is another goal of the book you are reading.

Conclusions

Obviously, more research needs to be conducted on almost every aspect of using graphic novels for enhancing literacy. More quantitative research is needed to show correlations between graphic novels and increased literacy skills. The theory, in other words, needs more practice. More qualitative data are needed as well. As yet, there is no study that thoroughly examines teachers' beliefs and attitudes concerning graphic novels; we have no clear idea of why teachers might be hesitant to use them. More success stories are needed, particularly via practitioner-based essays detailing use of graphic novels in actual classrooms. Furthermore, personal experience indicates that advocates of literacy and advocates of graphic novels need to come together to further the success of the format and the success of students employing it in their learning. In the meantime, in order to promote most effectively the impressive possibilities of the graphic novel for the English language arts classroom, teachers and scholars must get out the message concerning what research does exist on graphic novels and literacy. Bit by bit, we can expand the Golden Age of the graphic novel in the domain of education. By reading the essays that follow and considering their use in your own classrooms, you are joining the contributors in entering that Golden Age. Enjoy!

Further Recommended Reading

Brenner, R. (2006, March/April). Graphic novel 101 FAQ. *The Horn Book Magazine*, 123–125.

Brown, B. (2001). Pairing William Faulkner's *Light in August* and Art Spiegelman's *Maus*. *Making American Literatures in High School and College: Classroom Practices in Teaching English, 31*, 148–55. Urbana, IL: NCTE. Retrieved (in PDF) October 13, 2003, from EBSCO, 1–7.

Esquivel, I. (2006). Graphic novels: A medium with a message. *The Journal of Media Literacy, 53*(2), 33–39.

Freire, P. (2000). Education for critical consciousness. In A. M. A. Freire and D. Macedo (Eds.), *The Paulo Freire Reader* (p. 86). New York: Continuum.

Loewenstein, A. F. (1998). Confronting stereotypes: *Maus* in Crown Heights. *College English, 60*, 396–420.

Middaugh, D. (2006). Reading manga, or how I learned to stop worrying and just love reading. *Random House Inc. 1*(1), 70–75.

Rudiger, H. M. (2006, March/April). Reading lessons: Graphic novel 101. *The Horn Book Magazine*, 126–134.

Schwarz, G. (2006). Expanding literacies through graphic novels. *English Journal, 95*(6), 58–64.

Ujiie, J., & Krashen, S. D. (1996). Comic book reading, reading enjoyment, and pleasure reading among middle class and chapter 1 middle school students. *Reading Improvement, 33*(1), 51–54.

Ulaby, N. (2005, February 14). Holy evolution, Darwin! Comics take on science. National Public Radio's *Morning Edition*. Retrieved February 22, 2005, from http://www.npr.org/templates/story/story.php?storyID=4495248

References

Albers, P. (2006). Imagining the possibilities in multimodal curriculum design. *English Education, 38,* 75–101.

Bitz, M. (2004). The comic book project: Forging alternative pathways to literacy. *Journal of Adolescent & Adult Literacy, 47,* 574–86.

Bruggeman, L. (1997, January). "Zap! Whoosh! Kerplow!" Building high-quality graphic novel collections with impact. *School Library Journal, 43*(1), 22–27.

Bucher, K. T., & Manning, M. L. (2004). Bringing graphic novels into a school's curriculum. *Clearing House, 78,* 67–72.

Buckingham, D. (Ed.). (1998). *Teaching popular culture: Beyond radical pedagogy.* London: UCL Press.

Cadiero-Kaplan, K. (2002). Literacy ideologies: Critically engaging the language arts curriculum. *Language Arts, 79,* 372–81.

Callahan, B. (Ed.). (2004). *The new Smithsonian book of comic-book stories.* Washington, DC: Smithsonian Books.

Carter, J. B. (2004). Textus/praxis. http://nmc.itc.virginia.edu/E-folio/1/EDIS542/2004Fall-1/cs/UserItems/jbc9f_555.html

Cary, S. (2004). *Going graphic: Comics at work in the multilingual classroom.* Portsmouth, NH: Heinemann.

CBS. (2005). Newest teaching tool: Comic books. Retrieved March 25, 2005, from http://www.cbsnews.com

Cohn, N. Emaki productions. Retrieved October 13, 2003, from http://www.emaki.com

Deasy, R. (Ed.). (2002). *Critical links: Learning in the arts and student academic and social development.* Washington, DC: Arts Education Partnership.

Deasy, R. (Ed.). (2004). *The arts and education: New opportunities for research.* Washington, DC: Arts Education Partnership.

DeCandido, K. R. A. (1990, March 15). Picture this: Graphic novels in libraries. *Library Journal, 115*(5), 50–55.

Dewey, J. (1916). Democracy and education:.An introduction to the philosophy of education (pp. 8–9). New York: Macmillan.

Dorrell, L., & Carrol, E. (1981). Spider-man at the library. *School Library Journal, 27*(10), 17–19.

Dyson, A. H. (1997). *Writing superheroes: Contemporary childhood, popular culture, and classroom literacy.* New York: Teachers College Press.

Eisner, E. W. (1998). What do the arts teach? *RSA Journal* No. 5485 2(4). London: RSA.

Farrell, E. (1966). Listen, my children, and you shall read . . . *English Journal, 55*(1), 39–45.

Fiske, E. (Ed.). (1999). *Champions of change: The impact of the arts on learning.* Washington, DC: Arts Education Partnership.

Freire, P., & Macedo, D. (1987). *Literacy: Reading the word and the world.* South Hadley, MA: Bergin & Garvey.

Frey, N., & Fisher, D. (2004). Using graphic novels, anime, and the Internet in an urban high school. *English Journal, 93,* 19–44.

Galley, M. (2004). Going "graphic": Educators tiptoe into realm of comics. *Education Week, 23,* 6.

Gallo, D. (2004). Bold books for innovative teaching. *English Journal, 93*(5), 119–24.

Gambrell, L. B., & Jawitz, P. B. (1993). Mental imagery, text illustrations, and children's story comprehension and recall. *Reading Research Quarterly, 28,* 264–76.

Giroux, H. (1992). Border crossings: Cultural workers and the politics of education. New York: Routledge.

Goldsmith, F. (2003). Spotlight on graphic novels—Graphic novels as literature. *The Booklist, 99,* 986–88.

Goodlad, J. I. (2004). *A place called school.* New York: McGraw-Hill.

Gorman, M. (2003). *Getting graphic! Using graphic novels to promote literacy with preteens and teens.* Worthington, OH: Linworth.

Greene, M. (1995). *Releasing the imagination: Essays on education, the arts, and social change.* San Francisco: Jossey-Bass.

Grillo, T. (2005, February). Reaching teens: Back to the future. *NEAToday,* 26–28.

Hughes, S. (2005, April 8). Comic book science in the classroom. National Public Radio's *Morning Edition.* Retrieved April 8, 2005, from http://www.npr.org

Ingram, P. (2003). Hooks for reluctant readers. *Education Week, 23*(13), 26.

International Visual Literacy Association. What is visual literacy? Retrieved October 15, 2003, from http://www.ivla.org/org_what_vis_lit.htm#definition

Krashen, S. D. (1996). *Every person a reader: An alternative to the California task force report on reading.* Culver City, CA: Language Education Associates.

Krashen, S. D. (2004). *The power of reading: Insights from the research* (2nd ed.). Westport, CT: Libraries Unlimited.

Lavin, M. R. (1998). Comic books and graphic novels for libraries: What to buy. *Serials Review, 24*(2), 31–46.

Leckbee, J. (2004). Response to "What activity has been most effective in assisting high school students to read successfully?" Teacher to teacher column, *English Journal, 93*(5), 21.

Liu, J. (2004). Effects of comic strips on L2 learners' reading comprehension. *TESOL Quarterly, 38,* 225–45.

Marsh, J., & Millard, E. (2000). *Literacy and popular culture: Using children's culture in the classroom.* London: Paul Chapman.

Mayer, R. E. (1999). Research-based principles for the design of instructional messages: The case for multimedia explanations. *Document Design, 1,* 7–20.

McCloud, S. (1999). *Understanding Comics.* New York: DC Comics.

Meacham, S. J., & Buendia, E.. (1999). Modernism, postmodernism, and post-structuralism and their impact on literacy. *Language Arts, 76,* 510–16.

Mendez, T. (2004, October 12). 'Hamlet' too hard? Try a comic book. *Christian Science Monitor.* Retrieved March 25, 2005, from http://www.csmonitor.com

Mitchell, J. P., & George, J. D. (1996). What do Superman, Captain America, and Spiderman have in common? The case for comic books. *Gifted Education International, 11,* 91–94.

Moore, A., & Gibbons, D. (1987). *Watchmen.* New York: DC Comics.

Morrison, T. G., Bryan, G., & Chilcoat, G. W. (2002). Using student-generated comic books in the classroom. *Journal of Adolescent & Adult Literacy, 45,* 758–67.

Murray, C. (1997). Reading comics: Narrative and visual discourse in comics. Paper presented at the Scottish Word and Image Group Conference. Retrieved November 30, 2003, from Http://www.dundee.ac.uk/english/swig/papers.htm.

Myers, M. (1996). *Changing our minds: Negotiating English and literacy.* Urbana, IL: NCTE.

NCTE. (2005). Multimodal literacies. Retrieved January 14, 2006, from http://www.ncte.org/about/over/positions/category/media/123213.htm

Reid, C. (2002). Asian comics delight U.S. readers. *Publishers Weekly, 249*(51), 26.

Schwarz, G. E. (2002). Graphic novels for multiple literacies. *Journal of Adolescent & Adult Literacy, 46,* 262–65. Retrieved (in PDF) October 13, 2003, from EBSCO, 1–4.

Smith, M. W., & Wilhelm, J. D. (2002). *Reading don't fix no chevys.* Portsmouth, NH: Heinemann.

Spiegelman, A. (1986). *Maus I. A survivor's tale.* New York: Pantheon.

Spiegelman, A. (1991). *Maus II. A survivor's tale.* New York: Pantheon.

Toppo, G. (2005, March 3). Teachers are getting graphic. *USA Today.* Retrieved March 11, 2005, from http://www.usatoday.com

Vygotsky, L. S. (1978). *Mind in society: The development of higher psychological processes.* Cambridge, MA: Harvard University Press.

Weiner, S. (2001). *The 101 best graphic novels*. New York: NBM Publishing.

Weiner, S. (2002). Beyond superheroes: Comics get serious. *Library Journal, 127*(2), 55–58.

Weiner, S. (2004). Show, don't tell: Graphic novels in the classroom. *English Journal, 94*(2), 114–17.

Wertham, F. (1954). *Seduction of the innocent*. New York: Rinehart.

Wilson, B. (1999). Becoming Japanese: Manga, children's drawings, and the construction of national character. *Visual Arts Research, 25*(50), 48–63.

Xu, S. H. (2005). *Trading cards to comics strips: Popular culture texts and literacy learning in grades K–8*. Newark, DE: International Reading Association.

2 Altering English: Re-examining the Whole Class Novel and Making Room for Graphic Novels and More

Douglas Fisher and Nancy Frey
San Diego State University

Introduction

Let's start with a question: What is the purpose of the English classroom today? This question leads to a series of questions: Why do we devote forty-eight to ninety minutes per day to this subject in middle school and high school? What do we hope to gain from this use of instructional time? It seems to us that this simple question is the source of significant confusion. Are we literature teachers? Are we reading teachers? Do we need to teach students to "read for information" or just how to read? Do we want our students to learn the classics and to love literature? Do we hope that our students will develop habits of the mind and then be able to read for pleasure on their own? Or do we try to do it all?

It's likely that your beliefs regarding the answer to the initial question influence the way you, as a teacher, use time in the English classroom. Our thoughts about the purpose of the English classroom may differ significantly from yours. Alternatively, our answer to this question may challenge some of your assumptions, or it may even validate what you already believe. We think of the English classroom as a place for students to develop their thinking skills. We do this through a variety of texts and genres. We devote our instructional time to developing students' thinking skills so that they can understand, learn from, and appreciate what they read. For us, it's not as simple as deciding between classics and graphic novels, or classics and informational texts, or classics and adolescent literature. For us, it's deciding about the purpose of the instruction.

Although Carol Jago (2000) has made a compelling case for teaching classics in the English classroom, we have a hard time thinking about the ways in which a whole class novel can address all of our students' needs. We've never met a student who started out reading at the grade 4 level and then improved to the grade 9 level simply by reading grade 9 books. That's not to say that we don't like the classics and don't use them in our teaching. We are just concerned about the use of the whole class novel, especially when it is assigned as homework to be read outside of the school day.

We also aren't convinced that focusing on one novel will allow us to teach our students the content standards. In California, for example, English teachers organize their instruction around the following five standards (http://www.cde.ca.gov/be/st/ss/enggrades9-10. asp):

- Word Analysis, Fluency, and Systematic Vocabulary Development. Students apply their knowledge of word origins to determine the meaning of new words encountered in reading materials and then use those words accurately in writing.

- Reading Comprehension (Focus on Informational Materials). Students read and understand grade level-appropriate material. They analyze the organizational patterns, arguments, and positions advanced.

- Literary Response and Analysis. Students read and respond to historically or culturally significant works of literature that reflect and enhance their studies of history and social science. They conduct in-depth analyses of recurrent patterns and themes.

- Writing Strategies. Students write coherent and focused essays that convey well-defined perspective and tightly reasoned argument. The writing demonstrates students' awareness of the audience and purpose. Students progress through the stages of the writing process as needed.

- Writing Applications (Genres and Their Characteristics). Students combine the rhetorical strategies of narration, exposition, persuasion, and description to produce texts of at least 1,500 words each. Student writing demonstrates a command of standard American English and research, organizational, and drafting strategies.

These standards require that we devote significant time to thinking, reading, and writing for a variety of purposes. It's not that easy to address these standards when assigning tasks from a whole class novel.

Teaching these standards requires that we establish new structures that make it possible to offer the range of materials used in the English classroom, including graphic novels.

Structuring the Classroom

Although the choice of materials we use is critical and serves as the focus of this essay, we'd like to consider first the structure of the classroom. English classrooms of yesteryear were not organized in such a way as to provide students with opportunities to read across texts and genres. We know that reading multiple genres and texts improves comprehension and critical thinking (e.g., Frey & Fisher, 2004; Hynd, 1999). As such, we recommend that class time be devoted to four interrelated activities: focus lessons, guided instruction, collaborative learning, and independent learning (Frey & Fisher, 2006). Taken together, these four structures are designed to ensure a gradual release of responsibility from the teacher to the student (e.g., Pearson & Fielding, 1991). In other words, this transition in degree of responsibility suggests that the teacher moves from assuming "all the responsibility for performing a task . . . to a situation in which the students assume all of the responsibility" (Duke & Pearson, 2004, p. 211). A variety of texts can be used during these structured instructional activities.

Focus Lessons

Although adolescents need structured time to apply new strategies and skills on their own, they must first be taught how to use those strategies and skills. We refer to this instructional time as the focus lesson. The focus lesson begins with the teacher noting the purpose of the lesson. We know that when the teacher identifies objectives and provides feedback, student learning increases (Marzano, Pickering, & Pollock, 2001). As the next step, the teacher models through demonstration— for example, by pausing during a reading to emphasize the parts of the text that offer examples of the stated purpose. The teacher can then "scaffold" or structure the instruction by asking questions and providing prompts to foster discussion and to check for understanding. During the entire focus lesson, the teacher observes students to determine who might need further specific instruction. As the focus lesson ends, the teacher reviews the lesson and explains how the students will practice this strategy or skill during guided instruction and collaborative learning.

Guided Instruction

During guided instruction, students with similar learning needs are gathered together in small groups for a short time to receive specific instruction from the teacher, using text that is carefully matched to their current skills and the stated purpose of the lesson. The aim of guided instruction is to deliver customized lessons based on recent assessment information. Typically, the teacher meets with two groups of three to five students per day for fifteen minutes each.

Collaborative Learning

While students with specific skill needs are working with the teacher in guided instruction groups, the rest of the class is engaged in collaborative learning. These groups are not based on skills or abilities, but they are purposefully planned to ensure that each group represents a range of skills and needs. The tasks of collaborative learning groups range from literature circles and book clubs (e.g., Daniels, 2002) to word study and vocabulary development (Blachowicz & Fisher, 2002), peer editing (Simmons, 2003), and reciprocal teaching (Palinscar & Brown, 1986). Students work together in small groups to complete tasks that extend their knowledge and skills relative to the purpose established during the focus lesson.

Independent Learning

The goal of all of our instruction is that students achieve a level of independence in using literacy strategies that makes it possible for them to express their own thoughts and ideas and to understand the thoughts and ideas of others. Marie Clay refers to this as "the high demand from the first days of school for children to read and write texts according to their competencies but always as independently as possible" (2001, p. 48). After all, our intent is to develop a set of skills in each student that ultimately can be used outside the presence of the teacher and the classroom. We know that each student's ability to engage in independent reading and writing, like all aspects of learning, is fostered through explicit instruction.

The Role of the Whole Class Classic Novel

Given the classroom structure that we have proposed and researched, it seems reasonable to reconsider the role of the whole class novel. How would a classic, such as Steinbeck's *Of Mice and Men*, be used across this structure? Could it be used in the focus lesson? Yes. But would it be the best piece of text to learn skills and strategies from? Maybe not. Why do we feel the need to use difficult texts when we are modeling and demonstrating? Why not reduce the level of text difficulty when students are learning new skills and strategies that their teachers are modeling?

Could a classic be used during guided instruction? For some students, perhaps. For others, no. The key to guided instruction is matching the text difficulty with the needs of the group as well as the purpose of the lesson. The same piece of text will not work for all of the groups. In fact, each group of three to five students may need a different text selection. We understand that this presents a significant challenge to the teacher; fortunately, exceptional school librarians have provided us with resources related to our content at different reading levels and told from different perspectives.

So, could the classic be used during collaborative learning? Again, yes, in some cases. Is that the best use of the text? If the class were divided into literature circles, one of the groups might be reading *Of Mice and Men* while other groups would be reading other texts. With peer support and peer conversations about the literature, it seems reasonable to suggest that students could use what they have learned from the focus lesson and guided instruction and "try it out" in these peer discussions.

What about using the classic for independent learning? Our answer would be no. We know that students need to select their own reading materials and engage in free voluntary reading (e.g., Pilgreen, 2000). If we really want our students to become lifelong readers, we need to ensure that they have the opportunity to do so and the choice to read what they find interesting (Fisher, 2004; Ivey & Broaddus, 2001). Of course, they can apply all of the skills and strategies that we have taught them during the focus lesson, guided instruction, and collaborative learning to the books and materials they have chosen for themselves.

Using Multiple Texts to Teach Complex Ideas

Have you thrown your hands in the air? Are you pulling your hair out asking, "What do they suggest I actually do in my classroom?" Good. To address those questions, let's look inside Ms. Scott's classroom. During the fall semester, Ms. Scott required that her students, all of whom qualify for free lunch and are members of traditionally underrepresented groups, read the following classics: *The Odyssey*, *I Know Why the Caged Bird Sings*, and *Romeo and Juliet*. She explained, "The kids in the rich schools were all reading these books, so I wanted my students to read them as well. I dragged them through three books in the whole semester—for what? I'm not sure that they learned one new skill for reading, or that they even liked to read anymore when we were finished. And you know what? I visited one of the rich schools to see how they were teaching these books, and their students didn't really know them much better."

During the spring term, Ms. Scott changed her classroom structure dramatically and focused on demonstrating, modeling, scaffolding, and then coaching her students through a gradual release of responsibility. This required that she change her text selections to match the structure. For example, Ms. Scott knew that she needed to provide her students with instruction on literary devices. During one week, she focused on mood and tone.

On one of the days, her focus lesson centered on several pages of the graphic novel *New York: The Big City* (Eisner, 2000). Her purpose in using this particular text was to provide her students with visual images and words used by the authors/artists to convey tone and mood. As they read each of the pages, the students identified the tone and mood. As they did so, Ms. Scott asked for their evidence: What information were they using to identify and name the mood and tone? For example, on one page, a woman was shown walking to the fire hydrant to collect some water to mix her baby's formula [see Figure 9.1 on page 135]. One of the students said that the mood was sad. Ms. Scott asked, "What evidence do you have that the author wanted to create a sad mood?" The student replied, "I don't know, it just makes me feel sad." Ms. Scott probed further, "Interesting. The author created a mood for you. He must have done something." To this, the student responded, "I guess it's in her eyes. You see her eyes, they're just looking away from the baby and into the pictures on the mirror. I think she's sad—I would be sad if that was my life."

On this day, she had time to meet with two small groups. She knew that the members of the first group performed far below grade level and struggled with the English content standards. For this group, she had selected the picture book *Faithful Elephants: A True Story about Animals, People, and War* (Tsuchiya, 1951). This is a very emotional piece about the deliberate killing of the animals in Tokyo's Ueno Zoo during World War II so that the animals did not escape and run wild through the city. Ms. Scott read the book aloud and then started again from the beginning. A number of students cried and blew their noses; then, as a class, they identified specific words the author had used to establish the mood and tone. They noted that the book started off as "hopeful" and moved through anger, fear, resignation, and a host of other emotions.

With her second group, Ms. Scott selected *In the Shadow of No Towers* by Art Spiegelman (2004) because she wanted to extend this group's understanding of the subtleties of mood and tone. She knew that each of the students in this group would understand the feelings of loss and anger, but she wanted them to dig even deeper into the tone and mood that that the authors/artists were creating. Ms. Scott knew that, if she asked her students to identify moods and tones using both visual and textual information, they would start to look for these same tones and moods in their own reading and writing.

While she met with the two groups, other groups of students were engaged with their book clubs. One group had read *Batman: Child of Dreams* (Asamiya, 2003). Few graphic novels capture mood and tone better than the Dark Knight. This Japanese manga version involves battling an imposter and resisting the allure of a drug that promises to grant all of the wishes in the dreams of the user. Another group met to discuss *The Yellow Jar: Two Tales from the Japanese Tradition* (Atangan, 2002). They were deep in discussion about how the mood changed when the protagonist used deception to marry the woman he loved. They noted how the story moved from happiness to despair when the lie came back to haunt the young couple. Other students were reading independently, at their desks or in beanbag chairs, while others were meeting with their group members and having lively discussions about the topics and contents of the books. The groups were invited to select a book from a list that Ms. Scott had compiled. The titles from her booklist can be found in Figure 2.1.

The group discussion of *The Scarlet Letter* suggested that they had focused on the tone of foreboding. As one of the students suggested, "This part right here reminds me of the picture of the subway train in the graphic novel. You just know something bad is gonna happen." This student had clearly made a connection between the graphic novel and the classic she was reading with her group. Several of her peers agreed. One of them said, "Yeah, the author is telling us to pay attention—stuff's gonna go down and it ain't good." A few minutes later, another student indicated that he kept feeling sad while reading the book. When asked for specific examples from the text, the student listed specific words and phrases from the text that created a sad mood for him. This student was

Asamiya, K. (2003). *Batman: Child of Dreams*. M. A. Collins (Ed.). New York: DC Comics.

Atangan, P. (2002). *The Yellow Jar: Two Tales in the Japanese Tradition*. New York: NBM.

Brontë, C. [1890]. *Jane Eyre*. New York: Crowell.

Cisneros, S. (1994). *The House on Mango Street*. New York: A. A. Knopf.

Hawthorne, N. [1957]. *The Scarlet Letter*. New York: E. P. Dutton.

Orwell, G. (1946). *Animal Farm*. New York: Harcourt, Brace and Company.

Satrapi, M. (2003). *Persepolis: The Story of a Childhood*. New York: Pantheon.

Figure 2.1. Book club selections related to mood and tone.

clearly identifying the somberness that scholars have noted in Hawthorne's work.

During their independent reading and writing, students were asked to construct their own short stories using mood and tone. Ms. Scott knew that using the literary elements in their own writing would help students learn to understand these devices at a personal level. As such, her writing task for this unit of study provided students with an opportunity to use what they had learned and practiced.

Using Multiple Texts to Teach for Critical Literacy

Now we're going to push your thinking a bit more. So far, we have made a case for altering the structure of your English classroom to include time for focus lessons, guided instruction, collaborative learning, and independent reading. One argument for changing how instruction is delivered is that it frees up space for nontraditional texts, especially graphic novels. We've described how Ms. Scott found a way to avoid the either/or choice of classic novels versus nontraditional texts. By using a classroom structure predicated on a model that allows for gradual release of responsibility, she found a way to use a range of both classic and graphic novels that she had selected to teach a set of literacy devices. Although some of the texts were nontraditional, the notion of teaching literary devices certainly was not.

So, what if your English classroom moved away from analytic literacy—an approach that stresses identifying the "right" answers, such as plot, theme, and character analysis—and toward critical literacy? For the last decade, English education has been experiencing growing pains not seen since the late nineteenth century. At that time, analytic literacy itself was being born, influenced in no small measure by the new admissions examinations of the Ivy League universities (Applebee, 1974).

Now, more than a century later, English education is redefining itself once again. Critical literacy—an approach that emphasizes the roles of both the reader and the text—is becoming more widely recognized in secondary schools. However, many English teachers still feel caught up in the *Sturm und Drang* of it all. Critical literacy seems like a good idea, but, after all, if students don't know about plot and theme, character analysis, and literary devices, how are they ever going to be able to read critically?

Our answer is that they won't be able to do so if analytic literacy is viewed as a prerequisite to critical literacy. We don't believe that critical literacy is reserved only for the "gifted" classes, for the above grade-level readers. On the contrary, the core of critical literacy emphasizes evaluation, recognition of bias, and issues of social justice. How can students recognize what and who are missing from a text if they are excluded from a conversation about that text in the first place?

We realize that many adolescents arrive in our English classrooms without the basic knowledge of plot and theme, character analysis, and literary devices. We do not believe that this knowledge is inconsequential or that analytic literacy should be sacrificed for critical literacy. Instead, we have found that elements of analytic literacy can be taught within a curriculum focused on critical literacy. Furthermore, we have discovered that the accessibility of graphic novels provides an excellent introduction into the integration of both of these important stances toward literacy. We offer the following examples:

Analytic Literacy Focus: Symbol and Allegory

Neil Gaiman's *Sandman* series is arguably one of the most respected graphic novels of the last two decades. This ten-volume series spans seventy-five chapters and tells the tale of the Endless family, a mystical brood of siblings named Dream, Destiny, Death, Destruction, Desire, Despair, and Delirium. Each of these godlike creatures oversees the realm for which he or she is named. The novel opens the door to a discussion of mythology and of our human need to worship those with powers greater than our own. The novel has been compared to Joyce's *Finnegan's Wake* and to all of the Dickens's serials. Gaiman's *Sandman* series is ideal for teaching structures using multiple texts because the beginning of each volume offers a synopsis of what has occurred before. The critical literacy focus here involves issues of power, reflection, transformation, and action (Freire, 1970; McLaughlin & DeVoogd, 2004).

Analytic Literacy Focus: Author's Voice

Few genres lend themselves to a discussion of the role of the author's voice better than autobiographies. The first-person point of view is recognizable to all readers and can be more accessible for struggling readers than the omniscient voice used in other narratives. Autobiographical works also lend themselves to several critical literacy principles, including positioning and repositioning (placing the reader in an unfamiliar position in order to consider the larger world), as well as to discussions on which voices are missing from the work. For example, a unit focused on these analytic and critical literacy principles might include *Persepolis* (Satrapi, 2003), the autobiography of a young girl growing up in Iran during the revolution. Another group of students could read *Blankets* (Thompson, 2005), an account of the author's childhood in a fundamentalist Christian community in Wisconsin. A third group might read and discuss *Epileptic* (David B., 2002), an English translation of a French graphic novel that tells of the author's chaotic childhood as the younger brother of Jean-Christophe, a child with a severe form of epilepsy. His parents are desperate for a cure and involve the entire family in an increasingly bizarre set of treatments peddled by quacks.

The unifying theme in these works is the influence of faith, whether in religion or medicine, and the costs and benefits to those involved. In addition, each of these autobiographical graphic novels is told from the point of view of childhood memories. What distortions might be present? What might other family members offer in contrast to the author's viewpoint?

These are samples of graphic novels that can be used in a variety of ways to promote analytic and critical literacies (see Figure 2.2). Note that we are not advocating the replacement of the whole class novel from the canon by a whole class graphic novel. Instead, we find that the possibility of using nontraditional texts such as graphic novels is naturally expanded when the structure of the English classroom is altered to include focus lessons, guided instruction, collaborative learning, and independent reading.

Conclusions

The practice of the whole class novel has given rise to the practice of whole class instruction—or perhaps it's the other way around? In any case, given the diversity of needs among adolescents in any secondary classroom, it is unlikely that one novel will meet the needs of all learners. English teachers have always known this, yet an alternative to whole

Graphic Novel	Analytic Literacy Focus	Critical Literacy Focus
Gaiman, N. (1989). *The Sandman Vol. 1: Preludes and Nocturnes.* New York: DC Comics. [Note: there are ten volumes in this series.]	Allegory and symbolism through myth; the human need for stories to explain the universe	Issues of power through reflection, transformation, and action
David B. (2002). *Epileptic.* New York: Pantheon.	Author's voice; elements of autobiography	Positioning and repositioning
Satrapi, M. (2003). *Persepolis: The Story of a Childhood.* New York: Pantheon.		
Thompson, C. (2005). *Blankets.* Marietta, GA: Top Shelf Comix.		

Figure 2.2. Using graphic novels to teach analytic and critical literacy.

class instruction has not been common in middle school or high school. We have proposed altering the structure of the English classroom to include whole class focus lessons, teacher-directed guided instruction for small groups, student-directed collaborative reading groups for book clubs, and independent reading time for books of the students' choice. This four-component structure makes it possible to give students access to both classics and graphic novels that can be used to encourage them to learn to read and write in increasingly complex ways. When more flexible grouping patterns are used, the opportunity for differentiation of texts emerges. These texts can include graphic novels as well as canonical ones—texts that encompass a range of student needs, as well as multiple purposes that include principles of both analytic and critical literacy.

References

Applebee, A. N. (1974). *Tradition and reform in the teaching of English: A history.* Urbana, IL: National Council of Teachers of English.

Blachowicz, C., & Fisher, P. (2002). *Teaching vocabulary in all classrooms* (2nd ed.). Upper Saddle River, NJ: Merrill/Prentice Hall.

Clay, M. M. (2001). *Change over time in children's literacy development.* Portsmouth, NH: Heinemann.

Daniels, H. (2002). *Literature circles: Voice and choice in book clubs and reading groups* (2nd ed.). Portland, ME: Stenhouse.

Duke, N. K., & Pearson, P. D. (2004). Effective practices for developing reading comprehension. In A. E. Farstrup & S. J. Samuels (Eds.), *What research has to say about reading instruction* (3rd ed., pp. 205–42). Newark, DE: International Reading Association.

Eisner, W. (2000). *New York: The big city*. New York: DC Comics.

Fisher, D. (2004). Setting the "opportunity to read" standard: Resuscitating the SSR program in an urban high school. *Journal of Adolescent & Adult Literacy, 48*, 138–51.

Freire, P. (1970). *Pedagogy of the oppressed*. New York: Continuum.

Frey, N., & Fisher, D. (2004). Using graphic novels, anime, and the Internet in an urban high school. *English Journal, 93*(3), 19–25.

Frey, N., & Fisher, D. (2006). *Language arts workshop: Purposeful reading and writing instruction*. Upper Saddle River, NJ: Pearson Merrill/Prentice Hall.

Hynd, C. R. (1999). Teaching students to think critically using multiple texts in history. *Journal of Adolescent & Adult Literacy, 42*, 428–36.

Ivey, G., & Broaddus, K. (2001). "Just plain reading": A survey of what makes students want to read in middle school classrooms. *Reading Research Quarterly, 36*, 350–77.

Jago, C. (2000). *With rigor for all: Teaching the classics to contemporary students*. Portsmouth, NH: Heinemann.

Marzano, R. J., Pickering, D. J., & Pollock, J. E. (2001). *Classroom instruction that works: Research-based strategies for increasing student achievement*. Alexandria, VA: Association for Supervision and Curriculum Development.

McLaughlin, M., & DeVoogd, G. (2004). Critical literacy as comprehension: Expanding reader response. *Journal of Adolescent & Adult Literacy, 48*, 52–62.

Palincsar, A. S., & Brown, A. L. (1986). Interactive teaching to promote independent learning from text. *The Reading Teacher, 39*, 771–77.

Pearson, P. D., & Fielding, L. (1991). Comprehension instruction. In R. Barr, M. L. Kamil, P. Mosenthal, & P. D. Pearson (Eds.), *Handbook of reading research* (Vol. II, pp. 815–60). Mahwah, NJ: L. Erlbaum.

Pilgreen, J. L. (2000). *The SSR handbook: How to organize and manage a sustained silent reading program*. Portsmouth, NH: Boynton/Cook.

Simmons, J. (2003). Responders are taught, not born. *Journal of Adolescent & Adult Literacy, 46*, 684–93.

Spiegelman, A. (2004). *In the shadow of no towers*. New York: Pantheon.

Tsuchiya, Y. (1951). *Faithful elephants: A true story about animals, people, and war*. Boston: Houghton Mifflin.

3 Showing and Telling History through Family Stories in *Persepolis* and Young Adult Novels

Marla Harris

Introduction

Adolescence has always been a time of negotiating one's place inside and outside the family. Recently, attention has been given in English language arts to the power of exploring notions of family in the classroom (Gaughan, 2001; Nieto, 2002; Milner & Milner, 2003). But events such as the 9/11 terrorist attacks and the war with Iraq have made young Americans both more aware of the world beyond the borders of the United States and more anxious about their futures and those of their families. This essay details a series of young adult novels for an interdisciplinary teaching unit, appropriate for a middle school literature or social studies class. All of these novels concern families surviving and resisting in circumstances that are as threatening and apocalyptic to them personally as 9/11. These are family stories in a second sense, too, since most are inspired by the writer's own experience or the experiences of the writer's family.

The plot of the family against the world is not new: the prototype may be Johann David Wyss's *Swiss Family Robinson* (1812), the classic novel about a family shipwrecked in the Pacific, later made into a film (Disney, 1960). But unlike *The Swiss Family Robinson*, survival in these more recent young adult novels is not about contriving ingenious inventions and facing down wild animals in an attempt to civilize the wilderness. Instead, it is about coping in an allegedly "civilized" society that has reverted to a state of savagery—in which belonging to the "wrong" gender, religion, race, ethnicity, social class, or political party may mean being subject to persecution and violence. Reading these novels can give students valuable insights into the destructiveness of stereotypes and prejudices.

To begin the unit, have the class read *Persepolis: The Story of a Childhood* (2003), Marjane Satrapi's extraordinary graphic novel memoir, in which she describes how the heroine Marji and her family find their comfortable lives in Tehran, Iran, dramatically disrupted by the Islamic Revolution of 1979.

Given the availability of well-written fiction for young adults, why, you might ask, introduce graphic novels into the classroom? First, for a number of students, the predominantly pictorial format allows them to enter into difficult subject matter more readily than they might otherwise. Second, the assignment provides a bridge between students' leisure reading, which for many middle school students includes graphic novels, and the required reading that they do in school. As Stephen Krashen (2004) argues, bringing popular culture texts, such as comic books, into the classroom can be an effective strategy to engage reluctant readers. Third, the range of content in today's graphic novels ensures that teachers can find texts that work well thematically with young adult novels. Finally, this teaching unit implicitly challenges those critics who regard the conventional novel and the graphic novel as rivals, championing one format over the other. Graphic novels incorporate verbal elements, just as "literature, insofar as it is written or printed, has an unavoidable visual component" (Mitchell, 2002, p. 95). An early and extreme example is Laurence Sterne's *Life and Opinions of Tristram Shandy, Gentleman* (1759–1767), in which Sterne inserts blank pages, black pages, marbled pages, and pages filled with squiggles.[1] By integrating graphic novels thoughtfully into the middle school curriculum, we can encourage students to appreciate different formats as complementary rather than mutually exclusive ways of telling stories.

Before Reading *Persepolis*

In order to prepare students for reading *Persepolis*, first have them take a few moments to write down what they already know, or think they know, about Iran. What famous persons, news events, or objects come to mind when they think of Iran? One of Satrapi's stated aims is to present an alternative perspective on the Middle East and on Iran in particular, different from that supplied by the Western media, so that "an entire nation should not be judged by the wrongdoings of a few extremists" (2003, Introduction, n.p.). After students share their initial impressions, collect these responses.

Next, students can complete a webquest assignment that will serve as a brief introduction to the Iranian history and culture behind *Persepolis* (later in the unit, they can do more research into any area that

interests them). In conjunction with this webquest, it is helpful to locate Iran on a world map. The assignment asks the students to imagine
that they are archaeologists and adventurers from the future. While
digging in what is now Iran, they uncover a miscellaneous assortment
of finds that they have to catalog, including a copy of a book called the
Koran, a scrap of an elaborate woven rug, a photograph labeled "Jimmy
Carter," a missile manufactured in Iraq, a black veil, gold jewelry from
a place near the Oxus River, and the foot of a stone bull. Navigating the
following websites, students try to determine the significance for Iranian history and culture of each of these finds.

> http://www.iranchamber.com/history/iran_iraq_war/
> iran_iraq_war1.php
>
> http://www.thebritishmuseum.ac.uk/compass
>
> http://www.womeninworldhistory.com/essay-01.html
>
> http://www.npr.org/news/specials/mideast/the_west
>
> http://www.jimmycarterlibrary.org/documents/
> hostages.phtml
>
> http://www.iranchamber.com/carpet/brief_history_
> persian_carpet.php
>
> http://www.art-arena.com/persep1.htm
>
> http://www.historyforkids.org/learn/islam/religion

Teachers may elect to have students simply locate the answers or they
may choose to present the information in a more creative way, time
permitting.

Finally, as part of the preparation for reading *Persepolis*, devote
one class period to a general discussion of the graphic novel—what it
is and what it looks like. Encourage students who are already fans to
bring in their favorite graphic novels from home. (An excellent source
of graphic novels for interested teachers is the public library.)

Reading *Persepolis*

Once students have completed the webquest, they will have discovered
the source of Satrapi's title. Persepolis, the name of the ancient and ru-
ined Persian capital city, conjures up a place that no longer exists, the
pre-Revolutionary Iran of Marji's childhood. Satrapi's project, like an
archaeological excavation, is one of reconstructing the past, although
the style of drawing and the fact that the text does not always progress
in chronological order give it a dreamlike quality, as opposed to an objective documentary account. *Persepolis's* post-Revolutionary Tehran is

Figure 3.1. Marji attempts to re-create her grandfather's water torture by taking an exceptionally long bath.

a nightmare, its streets rendered unfamiliar and inhospitable first by hostile fundamentalists and later by foreign bombs. In order to survive physically, Marji and her family must conform outwardly, but to survive psychologically they must continue to resist.

As a graphic novel, Satrapi's narrative is inseparable from her art. Pairing child-like, literal drawings (see Figure 3.1) with matter-of-fact narration allows Satrapi to recreate horrific and violent events in an almost comic way, as when Marji seeks to re-create her grandfather's water torture by taking an exceptionally long bath, or when she imagines a dismembered body to be neatly sliced, without blood, bone, or tissue, resembling a doll rather than a mutilated corpse.

At other times, Satrapi's illustrations—for instance, those of Iranian cars fleeing Iraqi missiles—become intricate and attractive designs, reminiscent of Persian carpets, that obscure the meaning of the pictures themselves, as if asking how we can depict, in words or in images, these horrendous things that should not be possible (see Figure 3.2). Satrapi answers her own question when she inserts a black panel to represent the death of Neda Baba-Levy, Marji's Jewish neighbor and playmate.[2]

After reading *Persepolis,* divide students into groups to read one of the following young adult novels, all of which involve the growing awareness by young narrators of a disjunction between private (home and family) and public (street, school, and society) that requires them to reinterpret what they think they know about other people, including their own families. In three of these novels, this shift in perspective is the direct result of a war or revolution that militarizes everyday life

Figure 3.2. An illustration of Iranian cars fleeing Iraqi missiles.

by subjecting ordinary persons to surveillance and punishment. In all of the novels, the narrators and their families are compelled to live double lives metaphorically, literally, or both.

Red Scarf Girl by Ji-li Jiang (1997; 285 pp.)

Ji-li Jiang's heroine traces a trajectory similar to that of Marji. Just as the Islamic Revolution turns Marji's world upside down, so the Chinese Cultural Revolution in 1966 brings an end to Ji-li's dreams of joining the Red Guard and results in her parents' losing their jobs and health, her father's imprisonment, and her elderly grandmother's humiliation. Marji takes pride in learning about her grandfather's princely birth and political imprisonment, but when Ji-li's finds out that her grandfather was a landlord, it becomes a source of shame that leads to her family's classification as "black," or disloyal to Chairman Mao, and therefore targeted for persecution. The Chinese revolutionaries, similar to their Iranian counterparts, regulate what people wear, speak, and read, punishing those who are not in compliance, however unwittingly, like the young man walking down the street who is stripped of his Western-style clothes by self-appointed student inspectors as Ji-li watches. The Jiangs destroy evidence of their own history by burning family photos and recycling heirloom robes into mop heads, but still they continue to be treated as enemies of the state. Despite the temptation to disown her family members and rehabilitate herself politically, Ji-li ultimately refuses to disentangle her fate from theirs.

Before We Were Free by Julia Alvarez (2002; 167 pp.)

In Alvarez's novel, set in the Dominican Republic in 1960–1961, Anita de la Torre's family is subjected to a double tyranny—under the political and economic grip of the dictator General Trujillo, whose ruthlessness extends to murder and rape, and, simultaneously, the social control of the Americans, who run Anita's school, where the teachers favor the lighter-skinned, English-speaking children and "the American kids make fun of the way we speak English" (2002, p. 2). The novel begins at Thanksgiving, itself a story of how European immigrants—the Pilgrims—redefined themselves as natives, as the first Americans, relegating the Native Americans, like the Dominicans in Alvarez's story, to the status of second-class citizens. As with Marji and Ji-li, Anita's political consciousness is awakened abruptly, in this case by the hasty departure of her extended family and the arrival of the secret police, who move into her family's compound to place her parents, siblings, and herself under house arrest. Having grown up naively believing that her family admired Trujillo, Anita comes to realize that her father, Papi, is plotting to assassinate Trujillo and that most of the adults she knows on the island are part of a political resistance movement to overthrow the government. This revelation alters Anita's understanding of who her family is and what it means to be a Dominican. When Anita's home is ransacked and her father imprisoned (and later killed), Anita and her mother are forced to disappear, to go into hiding in the walk-in closet of their neighbors' bedroom, enduring a different kind of imprisonment.

Roll of Thunder, Hear My Cry by Mildred Taylor (1997; 276 pp.)

At first glance, it might seem that Taylor's novel about an African American family in Depression-era Mississippi does not belong with the other novels in this unit. The Logans, after all, experience no abrupt upheaval, no war or revolution; instead, the unnatural social conditions that are the remnants of slavery have become normalized to the point of being accepted by victims and victimizers alike. More dramatically, while Marji's ancestors were rulers, Cassie's were slaves. Yet Marji and Cassie and their families experience similar persecution. Just as secular Iranian families, like the Satrapis, dress and behave in certain ways in order to appease the judgmental religious fundamentalists who have seized political power, so the Logans are expected to conform to the local white community's stereotyped image of African Americans (see Figure 3.3). Otherwise, they may face violent consequences, such as being lynched.

While Marji courts punishment by mimicking "Western" girls, exchanging her veil and chador for denims and listening to Michael Jackson's music, the Logans place themselves at risk by acting white, that is, daring to assert themselves by educating their children, owning land, and boycotting the local white store for cheating sharecroppers. Like the white-run educational system that delivers separate and un-equal education and fires Mary Logan for teaching the truth, the legal system is willing to execute the Logans's neighbor, T. J. Avery, for a murder he did not commit rather than prosecute white boys.

Under the Blood-Red Sun by Graham Salisbury (1994; 246 pp.)

Salisbury's novel, set in Hawaii in 1941, is unique in this group of nov-els because it features a hero, Tomikazu (Tomi) Nakaji, rather than a heroine. Tomi's Japanese American family is ostracized and persecuted after the Japanese bombing of Pearl Harbor.[3] Born in Hawaii, Tomi achieves an uneasy balance between being an average American teen-ager and being a traditional Japanese boy. While his grandfather mocks his English speech and his white friends, white neighbors such as Keet Wilson label him a foreigner. After the Pearl Harbor attack, merely look-ing Japanese is enough to brand his family as potential Japanese spies: American pilots shoot and arrest his father, Mrs. Wilson fires Tomi's mother, and Mr. Wilson threatens Tomi with a gun. Like the Jiangs, the Nakajis try to hide pieces of their history that could incriminate them. Tomi explains, "We buried all our Japan things," including a Japanese flag and a samurai sword (p. 159). But when the FBI abruptly takes Tomi's grandfather away, Tomi rescues the samurai sword, which sig-nifies his refusal to renounce his Japanese-born family and his own iden-tity and which gives him the courage to stand up, finally, to the bully-ing Keet.

Figure 3.3. Marji and her classmates mourn the war dead in a mandated show of grief.

Conclusions

Graphic novels can be envisioned as supplementary materials, not as replacements for the young adult fiction that is already taught in the middle school classroom. The advantages of teaching graphic novels range from providing a fresh way of discussing traditional literary concepts, such as point of view, to bolstering students' own expertise as graphic novel readers, to reaching those students who have not enjoyed reading thus far. For teachers themselves, incorporating graphic novels can help refresh and revise classroom syllabi by suggesting new ways of juxtaposing texts.

Class presentations, discussions, and writing assignments should prompt students to make connections among the five novels, as well as to consider connections between the texts and their own lives. Although these "family stories" share the explicit aim of recording the experiences of a particular era, they do not belong simply to the realm of history, but touch on universal themes that may resonate with middle school students, who are rethinking their relationships within their own families. Adolescence is a period when the pressure to conform is great, and it can be socially risky to stand out as different or to stand up for something or somebody. Not only are there individual bullies in these novels, but institutions and governments that act like bullies, labeling people in order to justify their social, economic, or political disenfranchisement. The families in these novels choose not to surrender their sense of identity or integrity. The authors raise questions that are still relevant today: What constitutes patriotism? How can we make sense of an unjust society? And the stories remind us all how fragile the freedoms are that we so easily take for granted.

Topics for Student Discussion and/or Writing

1. Before reading *Persepolis,* write down your impressions and associations with Iran. Afterward, you can discuss whether your views have changed, and, if the answer is yes, specifically how they have changed.

2. Marji's family faces persecution partly because they do not share the religious beliefs of those in power. White families in Taylor's novel do not see their churchgoing as incompatible with harassing the Logans and other African American families. What is the relationship between religious observance and moral behavior in each novel? Is there any correlation?

3. Marji goes along with her friends when they "cut" school, T. J. Avery joins his white "friends" in robbing a store, Billy Davis temporarily turns on Tomi, and Ji-li is pressured into denouncing her teachers. What kinds of peer pressure are evident in each novel? How is the peer pressure that they experience like or unlike peer pressure in your middle school? There are also examples of mobs in *Persepolis*, *Red Scarf Girl*, and *Roll of Thunder*. Ji-li herself is at first an enthusiastic participant in a mob that destroys shop signs. How do people act differently in large groups than they might in other circumstances, both in these novels and in your own experience?

4. Examine how specific colors are used in these novels. Discuss the meanings attached to black, white, red (in *Red Scarf Girl*), purple (in *Before We Were Free*), and any other colors that you notice. Make a color chart, listing people, objects, and adjectives under each color.

5. *Persepolis* has deceptively simple black-and-white drawings. Would the novel as a whole be different with drawings in color? Why do you think Satrapi chose to use only black and white? Does it seem appropriate or not? Explain.

6. In each novel, schools are temporarily suspended, permanently closed, or transformed in some way as a result of political and social events. How do schools resist or reflect the politics and prejudices of the society around them in each case? To what extent are students of different social classes, races, or ethnic backgrounds segregated, officially or unofficially?

7. Each novel is told from one character's point of view. The second panel of Satrapi's novel purports to show Marji's class, but it deliberately "crops" Marji's picture: "I'm sitting on the far left so you don't see me" (2003, p. 3). The veil, in fact, is a perfect symbol for the narrator, allowing someone to see without being seen. In what way is each narrator not only an observer or reporter of events, but also an editor?

8. Even though most of these novels are told from a female point of view, each novel, apart from *Persepolis*, also includes boys as important characters. Giving specific examples to support your opinion, do you think it is more difficult to be a boy or girl in each book? Ironically, Anita's brother Mundin masquerades as a girl to flee the country, while her sister Lucinda is endangered precisely because she is a pretty girl who has attracted the attention of Trujillo. What different kinds of dangers do boys and girls face in these novels?

9. One way that repressive governments exert control is through censorship, which may be violent, as in the destruction of Hong's bookstall in *Red Scarf Girl*, or more subtle, as in the outdated and biased history textbooks supplied to the Great Faith School in *Roll of Thunder*. Can you find other examples of censorship in these novels? The United States is not immune to censorship; even Laura Ingalls Wilder's *Little House on the Prairie* has been attacked as unsuitable. Find a list of targeted books (http://www.ala.org/ala/oif/bannedbooksweek/bbwlinks/100most frequently.htm). Have you read any of these books? Do you agree in principle with censoring books? If so, under what circumstances?

10. Although these novels are not about slavery, they all contain examples of persons being unfairly imprisoned and, in some cases, executed. Even when characters are not in literal prisons, they are not wholly free when it comes to speech, education, travel, jobs, and dress. One of the novels, *Before We Were Free*, explicitly mentions freedom in its title. To what extent is this title applicable to the other novels?

11. Mary Logan defiantly pastes over the inside front covers of school texts and organizes a boycott, Stacey Logan plots revenge on the white school bus by digging a ditch in the muddy road, and Marji talks back to her teachers. In *Persepolis*, subtle signs acquire political meaning (see Figure 3.4): "You showed your opposition to the regime by letting a few strands of hair show" (Satrapi, 2003, p. 75). Anita's erasing her diary entries as soon as she has written them and Tomi's refusal to kill his last two pigeons are private gestures of protest. As a class, make a list of all of the different strategies of resistance employed by individual characters. Are some more successful than others? More satisfying?

12. The characters in these novels are forced to lie in order to protect themselves and others. As Marji says, "I learned to lie quickly" (Satrapi, 2003, p. 75). She lies to the woman who threatens to turn her in for wearing Western clothes, but she also lies to her mother about playing hooky from school. Are there different kinds of lies? In what kinds of situation is lying acceptable or even heroic? Are there times in these novels when telling the truth endangers other people?

13. After finishing *Persepolis*, speculate on what you think will happen to Marji in boarding school in Vienna (in 2004, Satrapi published a sequel entitled *Persepolis 2: The Story of a Return*). How will she fit in? Will she miss her family? What kinds of challenges might she face?

Figure 3.4. A lighthearted example of resistance in *Persepolis.*

14. In the course of each novel, the idea of "home" as a safe refuge is put into question. Marji's family must deal with continual bombings as well as the possibility of surprise searches, Anita's family is placed under house arrest when the secret police move in, Ji-li's family is subjected to raids on their apartment, and Cassie's family lives in fear of nighttime "home invasions" by white vigilantes. Even Anita's grandparents' New York apartment is "watched" by the doorman; Anita must pretend not to live there because "it's sort of illegal that we're staying in their rooms with them" (Alvarez, 2002, p. 140). How does the attitude toward home change through each novel? Several of these characters, like their authors, ultimately leave their home or their homeland. How do they feel? How does Tomi's grandfather feel about having left Japan?

15. Language itself can be deceptive, deliberately hiding meanings. As a class, create an ongoing "dictionary" of the "code" words, slang, or jargon in each novel. In some cases, as with "fourolds," re-labeling ordinary objects demonizes them; in other cases, dangerous or menacing objects, such as guns, are made innocuous through their renaming as "ingredients" for a "picnic."

16. Grandparents occupy a special position in each novel, although they are not always idealized. Tomi, for instance, has a difficult relationship with his grandfather. Describe the relationships between the grandparents and their grandchildren who are the heroes and heroines of the novels. Describe the role played by grandparents in each story.

Student Activities and Projects

1. Letters are often more than just a means of communication in these novels, where there is a danger of private letters becoming public or being read by the wrong people. Marji's father is furious to discover that she has written love letters for her illiterate maid Mehri; the ghostwritten letters symbolize Mehri's overstepping her boundaries as a lower-class woman. Ji-li's home is ransacked and her father arrested after officials learn about an incriminating letter. The personal letters that pass between Anita and her sister in the United States are treated as suspicious documents. Select a character from one of the books that you have read and write a letter to Marji in *Persepolis*, offering advice, based on that character's own experience.

2. Each of these novels concerns a historical era with which you are likely to be unfamiliar. Research either an aspect of *Persepolis*, such as the Iranian hostage crisis or the fate of the last Shah, Reza Pahlavi, or an aspect of the second book that you have read, such as the Chinese Cultural Revolution, the so-called Jim Crow laws, or the treatment of Japanese Americans during World War II. You might share this research with the class in the form of a short paper, a PowerPoint presentation, or even a short original graphic novel.

3. In *Mississippi Bridge* (1990), the Logans's white neighbor, Jeremy Simms, is the narrator. How would each of these novels be different if told from another point of view? If the narrator were of another social class, race, or generation? In *Before We Were Free*, would Chucha, the eccentric and superstitious family housekeeper, describe what happens differently? What if Anita's American neighbor Sam Washburn, an outsider in the Dominican Republic, were telling the story? What if Ji-li's grandmother were narrating the events of *Red Scarf Girl*? What if Mehri, the Satrapis's maid, whose romance is brutally ended by Marji's father and who is slapped by Marji's mother, were the narrator of *Persepolis*? Or Nada Baba-Levy, the Jewish girl who is killed when a bomb destroys her house? How would Billy Davis relate what happens after the attack on Pearl Harbor? Rewrite a scene or episode from any of the assigned novels as a diary entry from the perspective of another character in that same novel.

4. Reading a graphic novel in class may lead logically to creating your own graphic novels.[4] For this assignment, draw panels and create text dramatizing one specific scene or episode from the young adult novel that you have read. Then you might write a brief description about how

your illustrated versions represent changes from the original novel. A discussion about the idea of adaptation might follow: novels, especially classic children's fiction, are often recast as plays, films, television series, and animated series, all of which require editing and rewriting. As you experiment with your own graphic novel versions, you will likely become more aware of these processes.

5. As another follow-up project, you might research your own family history, by talking to relatives or by online searching. Select an episode that might then be presented either in the form of an oral history or, again, as an excerpt from a graphic novel. Each of the families in these novels makes a decision not to leave. The family histories of most Americans begin with an ancestor, maybe even a parent or grandparent, leaving his or her homeland to come to the United States. If this is true in your family, what do you know about those who stayed behind? What was life like for those who came to the United States?

6. You might devise your own webquests for the young adult novel that you are reading and present them to the class.

7. The past figures significantly in each novel. Satrapi's great-grandfather was an emperor, and her grandfather a political prisoner; Cassie's great-grandfather Logan was a white slave-owner, and her grandfather a free landowner; and Ji-li's grandfather was a landlord. Land is a valuable legacy in more than one of these novels, but so are other more portable possessions. Write a story about a cherished object belonging to a family member, such as Tomi's grandfather's samurai sword, Ji-li's grandmother's chest of clothes, or Anita's Dominican-map eraser.

Recommended Websites about Graphic Novels:

http://www.noflyingnotights.com (Robin Brenner)

http://ublib.buffalo.edu/lml/comics/pages/reading.html (Michael R. Lavin)

http://www.informationgoddess.ca/Comics&GraphicNovels/index.htm (Janice Biebrich)

Articles about *Persepolis*:

Kapoor, Mini. "It's Graphic, But Is It a Novel?" Rev. Marjane Satrapi, *Persepolis. The Indian Express.* Retrieved October 10, 2004, from http://www.indianexpress.com/res/web/pIe/print.php?content_id=56549

Pantheon discussion guide for Marjane Satrapi, *Persepolis*. http://www.randomhouse.com/pantheon/catalog/display.pperl?isbn=0375422307&view=rg

Satrapi, Marjane. "On Writing Persepolis." Interview with Pantheon. http://www.randomhouse.com/pantheon/graphicnovels/satrapi2. html

Storace, Patricia. "A Double Life in Black and White." Review of *Persepolis: The Story of a Childhood*; *Persepolis 2: The Story of a Return*, by Marjane Satrapi. Trans. L'Association, Paris, France. *New York Review of Books*, April 7, 2005: 40–43.

Notes

1. For the ways that typography influences how we read, see *Illuminating Letters: Typography and Literary Interpretation*, eds. Paul C. Gutjahr and Megan L. Benton (Amherst: U. of Massachusetts, 2001).

2. This black panel has precedents as far-ranging as *Tristram Shandy* (where Sterne uses it to mark the death of the fictional Yorick) and Art Spiegelman's *New Yorker* cover for the week of 9/11.

3. Interested students may wish to read *Farewell to Manzanar* (1976), Jeanne Wakatsuki Houston and James D. Houston's poignant account of life in a Japanese American internment camp in California during World War II, or *The Journal of Ben Uchida (My Name is America)* by Barry Denenberg (New York: Scholastic, 1999).

4. There are several recent books about creating graphic novels, including Mike Chinn's *Writing and Illustrating the Graphic Novel: Everything You Need to Know to Create Great Graphic Works* (Hauppauge, NY: Barron's Educational Series, 2004).

References

Alvarez, J. (2002). *Before we were free*. New York: Alfred A. Knopf.

Gaughan, J. (2001). A literary transfusion: Authentic reading-writing connections. In B. O. Ericson (Ed.), *Teaching reading in high school English classes* (pp. 33–47). Urbana, IL: NCTE.

Jiang, J. (1997). *Red scarf girl: A memoir of the cultural revolution*. New York: HarperTrophy.

Krashen, S. D. (2004). *The power of reading: Insights from the research*. Westport, CT: Libraries Unlimited.

Milner, J., & Milner, L. F. M. (2003). *Bridging English* (3rd ed.). Upper Saddle River, NJ: Merrill/Prentice Hall.

Mitchell, W. J. T. (2002). Showing seeing: A critique of visual culture. In N. Mirzoeff (Ed.), *The visual culture reader* (2nd ed., pp. 86–101). New York: Routledge.

Nieto, S. (2002). *Language, culture, and teaching: Critical perspectives for a new century.* Mahwah, NJ: L. Erlbaum.

Salisbury, G. (1994). *Under the blood-red sun.* New York: Dell Laurel-Leaf.

Satrapi, M. (2003). *Persepolis: The story of a childhood.* New York: Pantheon.

Taylor, M. D. (1990). *Mississippi bridge.* New York: Dial Books for Young Readers.

Taylor, M. D. (1997). *Roll of thunder, hear my cry.* New York: Puffin.

4 Are There Any Hester Prynnes in Our World Today? Pairing *The Amazing "True" Story of a Teenage Single Mom* with *The Scarlet Letter*

James Bucky Carter
University of Virginia

Legacies

Nathaniel Hawthorne's *The Scarlet Letter* has long been a high school classic. The chronicles of Hester Prynne's hardships at the hands of her neighbors and her attempts to make a decent life for herself and her daughter Pearl, in the face of social banishment and without the explicit help of the child's father, have been explored in English classrooms for generations as symbolic of the intolerance and hypocrisy of seventeenth-century American Puritans.

Throughout those generations, scores of young women (today, roughly fifty-one teens per thousand, according to The Women's Health Channel, www.womenshealthchannel.com) have given birth themselves and raised their children under difficult circumstances. For them, Hester's personal experiences are not highly symbolic, but matter-of-fact actualizations of everyday life. Similar to Hester's ostracized condition, the place that single and teenage mothers have long held in public education is dubious: they are often forced out of school or "hidden away" from the view of other students. Elizabeth Ann Poe recognized this in "Alienation from Society in *The Scarlet Letter* and *The Chocolate War*," which appeared in *Adolescent Literature as a Complement to the Classics* (Kaywell, 1993): "When I used this novel with a class of pregnant teens and teenage mothers . . . they read *The Scarlet Letter* with enthusiasm and sympathy . . . due to their own painful experiences, they understood the alienation of Hester Prynne" (p. 185).

Even in the twenty-first century, teenage pregnancy is considered a taboo subject, but when it is discussed, allusions to Hester are often not far away. In 2000, for example, an initiative by the National Campaign to Prevent Teen Pregnancy resulted in advertisements featuring "wayward appearing teens behind large red letters spelling out CHEAP, DIRTY, NOBODY, REJECT, USELESS, or PRICK; with smaller captions below stating 'sex has consequences'" (Constantine & Benard, 2000). Critics saw these as attempts to guilt and shame students into abstinence and labeled them "the *Scarlet Letter* ads" (see Figure 4.1 and more of the images at websites listed in the References section of this essay). The *Christian Science Monitor* reported, "Despite greater acceptance in some circles, these young mothers find that the scarlet letter still exists. In their case, the A stands for adolescent pregnancy" (Gardner, 2004). Columnist *Adrienne Donnell* recently defended pop singer and single mother Fantasia Barrino and her song "Baby Mama":

> She is shaping the hope of these young mothers to believe in themselves and to move forward with their lives. That is proven in the line from the song where she says, "We can go anywhere, we can do anything. I know we can make it if we dream." By no means is she condoning premarital sex. It is reality and it is happening. We cannot brand them with a scarlet letter on their forehead, throw them in a closet and pretend that this isn't happening." (Donnell, 2005).

When I began my research for this essay in March 2005, an informal Web search using "the Scarlet Letter" and "teenage pregnancy" netted 480 items. Teenage mothers and *The Scarlet Letter* are now more inextricably linked than ever, and high school teachers may need to explore the concepts surrounding them in tandem and touch on social issues that deter students from "remember[ing] it with dismay" (Poe, 1993, p. 185). Lorraine Cella (2002) tackles these concurrent issues head-on in her English classroom. She asks students to "search their current belief systems and thoughts prior to reading *The Scarlet Letter*" via these two poignant sets of questions:

> Boys: Imagine you have a child and are not married to the mother. What would you feel is your responsibility? What would your family, friends, and members of the community think about you? What about your background makes you think as you do?

> Girls: Imagine you have a child and are not married to the father. What would your family, friends, and the community think about you? What about your background makes you think as you do? (p. 78).

Figure 4.1. One of the ads developed by the National Campaign to Prevent Teen Pregnancy.

Teachers may want to use these questions to initiate class discussions or let them be guides for developing their own approaches for teaching *The Scarlet Letter* in conjunction with talking about teen pregnancy. In addition, this essay offers a further means to accomplish the overall objective: pairing *The Scarlet Letter* with a more contemporary novel that explores similar ideas. Alienation is a natural theme of the two texts, although the similarities do not end there.

Katherine Arnoldi's autobiographical graphic novel *The Amazing "True" Story of a Teenage Single Mom* (1998)[1] is a "pictorial memoir of one young woman's journey from childhood to adulthood via an unplanned pregnancy at 17 years of age," which portrays "the harsh realities that often face a teenage mom" (Gorman, 2003, p. 27). Michele Gorman says of the text that it is a "poignant, yet honest story of love, loss, hurt, birth, rebirth, and renewal" and that it is "likely to spark a conversation in any high school classroom" (p. 27). *The Amazing "True" Story of a Teenage Single Mom* details Arnoldi's attempts to escape poverty, abuse, and social stratification as a young mother. This graphic novel is a perfect pairing with Nathaniel Hawthorne's classic, *The Scarlet Letter*. Indeed, toward the end of her narrative, Arnoldi adds validation to comparisons of the inherent difficulties of teen pregnancy and of Hester Prynne's circumstances (see Figure 4.2).

Pairing the Texts

Katherine is truly a modern-day Hester in her text, and so teachers can easily draw parallels between the two. A comparison of the connection the author feels between herself and her daughter Stacie and Hawthorne's account of the relationship between Hester and Pearl can act as an excellent springboard for class discussion. Teachers may want to help students to note the following:

- Hester feels ostracized; similarly, Katherine's mother and other relatives disown her.

- Just as Hester faces public humiliation and must struggle to make ends meet, Katherine works dead-end jobs that leave her sick with pneumonia and lives from paycheck to paycheck.

- Men are portrayed as despicable characters in both novels. Reverend Dimmesdale is a weak-willed man of little resolve; Stacie's father is an anonymous rapist; and Hester's husband Chillingworth is an evil, decrepit alchemist who is often associated with the demonic. Katherine's misogynistic patrons at the restaurant where she waitresses, her nameless brother-in-law who sexually abuses her, and her physically violent live-in boyfriend Dave (see Figure 4.3) are all drawn as lascivious, hideous-looking demons.

- Katherine invokes the help of her father, whom she has never met but whose name she remembers from some old luggage her family used to own. But she discovers that he is a self-important braggart who offers little help before quickly abandoning her for the second time. Likewise, Hester's heavenly father seems to offer her little help as she struggles through her harsh life. As student Emily said of *The Scarlet Letter* in L. F. Bassett's English class, "All of them, the men, I mean, think it's about them" (Bassett, 1998, p. 65). Katherine deals with similar masculine arrogance.

Figure 4.2. Arnoldi identifies herself as a modern Hester Prynne.

- Hester comes to see escape to a different society as a means to better her daughter's situation; similarly, Katherine finds hope in moving "out West."
- Getting a college education eventually becomes Katherine's analogue to Hester's sewing, a method of gaining legitimacy in the larger society as well as a means by which to provide for her daughter.

That Arnoldi's tale is her own autobiographical story is important to note. Pairing an autobiography with *The Scarlet Letter* will add to the students' notions of Hester's humanity. Furthermore, Arnoldi speaks from a personal experience that Hawthorne could not have: she's a woman. As sympathetic as Hawthorne is toward Hester, he could never feel her hardship the way another woman could. He could never be a teenage mother. Pairing the Arnoldi work with the classic text can, on the one hand, help emphasize the value of Hawthorne's superb writing skills or, on the other, lead to debates about whether Hawthorne was truly able to do justice to Hester's plight. Furthermore, although only a handful of students, if any, in a given class can directly relate to being unwed mothers, discussing Pearl and Stacie, the children of the leading females, can create personal connections with the stories. (Even as a male, I can only sympathize with Hester, as does Hawthorne, via my imagination. However, as the first child of a teenage and, later, a single

Figure 4.3. Dave reacts to Katherine's idea of applying to college.

mother, I feel immediate and personal connections to Hester, Rose, Katherine, and Stacie, and I'm sure there are many students who can do so as well).

Of course, there are significant differences between the two texts that must be considered. Katherine is able to escape via travel, whereas Hester is impeded in her efforts. Hester's daughter Pearl, however, does go abroad and is able to live a comparatively easier life than her mother, at least. Although both authors manage to demonstrate some acceptable qualities in men such that neither text can legitimately be called sexist, helpful male characters in Arnoldi's text play quite minor roles: the male truck drivers who invoke Katherine's gratitude for helping her travel cross-country. On the other hand, Hawthorne's Dimmesdale, who eventually finds his backbone and fesses up (although perhaps drugged or mentally ill when he does so), is a main character in the novel. Unlike Hester, Katherine has a strong female friendship—with her roommate Debbie—that sustains her at certain times, and she eventually finds support from Jackie, who teaches her how to apply to college and how to request financial aid. She also finds a free day care situation for Stacie that offers her the support of an accepting community, something that Hester can never find.

The Amazing "True" Story of a Teenage Single Mom ends more happily than *The Scarlet Letter*, and teachers can use this fact to discuss the changes in our society since Hester's era. Students may conclude that contemporary society is more accepting of teenage mothers, which leads, inevitably, to a discussion of questions that explore current sensibilities about teenage mothers and that challenge students to better understand their situation. A Web search for articles on teen pregnancy can help teachers make the case that the Katherines and Hesters of today still struggle.

Further distinctions must be made between the circumstances of the two women. Hester is an unwed mother and an adulterer, but she may or may not be a teenager. Katherine is an unwed teenager, but she does not knowingly commit adultery (the details of the rapist's life are unknown to the reader and, most probably, to Arnoldi herself). Teachers can play these circumstances off of one another to encourage students to decide who had a rougher go of it in the novels or, better yet, who has a rougher go of it today—the unwed mothers, adulterers, pregnant teens, or some combination thereof. If media materials are used in the classroom, as in this essay, to pair Hester's red letter with Katherine's teen pregnancy, clarification should be made concerning conflated differences between unwed mothers, adulterers, and teenage mothers.

Guiding Questions

The following questions can guide teachers in exploring both works more critically. Many of them can easily be reconstructed as writing prompts or used in connection with certain panels of the graphic novel (using an overhead projector or photocopies). Teachers may consider bringing in copies of the "the *Scarlet Letter* ads" for heightened visual effect and comparison. In addition, teachers may want to integrate health education information and statistics on teenage pregnancy into the discussion. Teachers needing more practical suggestions for teaching the theme of alienation in the two novels should see Poe's essay (Kaywell, 1993).

- Katherine talks about being considered a person who has "made her bed." What does this mean? How does this phrase show itself in *The Scarlet Letter*?
- Hester is disowned by the town once her condition is made public. Katherine too is disowned in many ways, as is shown

throughout the text. Discuss the differences and similarities within the theme of "abandonment" in relation to the two women.

- In what ways do both Hester and Katherine face ridicule and rejection?

- Katherine depicts men in various forms, based on her connection to them and their true inner selves. Which of the men in *"True" Story* might Chillingworth and Dimmesdale most resemble, and why?

- Study the images from Arnoldi's text shown in Figure 4.3. Do you recognize them? [Help students to recognize a given image, such as the one of Dave, as one of the men in the text.] Can you make a case for these images to be photographs of a character from *The Scarlet Letter*? Explain your rationale.

- Why do you think Katherine raises her hand in the panel where she is studying *The Scarlet Letter* in college?

- Travel is a major theme in both books, but at different times. How is travel important in the two texts?

- What is the significance of travel as escape? How is the idea of "escape" approached and resolved differently in the two texts?

- Before beginning her story, Arnoldi states that she created the book to "take to GED (high school equivalency) programs" to "help single moms feel worthy to pursue their rights to an equal access to education and provide them with the information to do so, since young moms often miss out on high school guidance counseling. That for me is the sole purpose of this book." How does this frame influence your perception of the story? Does Hawthorne's "custom house" frame do as much to influence your interpretation of his story as does Arnoldi's?

- Which of the two texts succeeds the most in educating its audience? Give evidence for your assertions.

- The back cover of *"True" Story* says that Arnoldi uses "a form usually reserved for superheroes conquering universes." But can the case be made that the form was well chosen because that's exactly what happens in the text? In fact, can Hester Prynne be seen as equally heroic, even if she didn't succeed in the way that Katherine was able to? Furthermore, did Arnoldi make the right decision to use the graphic novel format to tell her story? Does using the comic book format make her story more powerful than it would have been in printed prose? Does the Arnoldi text's use of this format make you rethink how you look at comic books and graphic novels?

- How are Katherine's and Hester's relationships with their daughters different?

- How are Pearl and Stacie depicted in the texts? Do they have more similarities or more differences? Why do you say what you said in response to these questions?

- How is Katherine's father similar to any of the characters in *The Scarlet Letter*? In terms of the religious nature of the Hawthorne text, can parallels be made between Katherine's father and God?

- Arnoldi gives us an inside look at Stacie's brain and at her own. Draw similar pictures detailing what's going on in Pearl's mind and in Hester's mind.

A Final Word

Pairing *The Scarlet Letter* with *The Amazing "True" Story of a Teenage Single Mom* can shed light on the tragedy of constricting and repressive norms that spring from community values, religious beliefs, or common perceptions. It can also help students to better understand a challenging novel, driving home the realities of Hester Prynne and figures like her, past and present. Often considered a stale American relic, *The Scarlet Letter* gains fresh relevance when coupled with Arnoldi's graphic novel autobiography.

Author's Note

As of this publication, I have been informed by Katherine Arnoldi that her book is no longer in print but can be purchased at Amazon.com or from the NOW website (http://www.now.org). In addition, the book is an American Library Award winner and should be found in most public libraries. A movie version is expected in theaters in about two years. If you enjoy her story, please feel free to visit her website at http://www.katherinearnoldi.com to let her know and to express interest in a possible paperback version, which would allow for inexpensive copies for classroom use.

References

Arnoldi, K. (1998). *The amazing "true" story of a teenage single mom*. New York: Hyperion.

Bassett, L. F. (1998). An English class with Emily. English Journal, *87*(3), 64–66.

Cella, L. (2002). Reading the complex world: Students approach *The Scarlet Letter* from multiple perspectives. *English Journal, 91*(6), 77–82.

Constantine, N., & Benard, B. (2000, November). "Dirty campaign?" *Youth Today*. Retrieved March 25, 2005, from http://crahd.phi.org/dirtycampaign.html

Donnell, A. (2005, February 19). Fantasia's "Baby Mama" drama. *Black Voice* (news online edition). Retrieved March 25, 2005, from http://www.blackvoicenews.com/modules.php?file=article&name=News&op=modload&sid=2862

Gardner, M. (2004, May 19). They change diapers and perception. *The Christian Science Monitor.* Retrieved March 26, 2005, from http://www.christiansciencemonitor.com/2004/0519/p11s01-lifp.html

Gorman, M. (2003). *Getting graphic: Using graphic novels to promote literacy with preteens and teens.* Worthington, OH: Linworth.

Hawthorne, Nathaniel. (1986). *The scarlet letter.* New York: Bantam Books.

Kaywell, J. F. (Ed.). (1993). *Adolescent literature as a complement to the classics.* Norwood, MA: Christopher-Gordon.

The National Campaign to Prevent Teen Pregnancy. Retrieved March 26, 2005, from http://www.teenpregnancy.org/

The National Campaign to Prevent Teen Pregnancy. Retrieved March 26, 2005, from http://www.teenpregnancy.org/contact/soundoff.asp

Poe, E. A. (1993). Alienation from society in *The Scarlet Letter* and *The Chocolate War.* In J. F. Kaywell (Ed.), *Adolescent literature as a complement to the classics.* Norwood, MA: Christopher-Gordon.

Women's Health Channel. Teen Pregnancy. Retrieved June 24, 2005, from http://www.womenshealthchannel.com/teenpregnancy/index.shtml

5 Visualizing Beowulf: Old English Gets Graphic

J. D. Schraffenberger
Binghamton University

Introduction

Beowulf clearly has historical and literary significance in English class-rooms. As a cultural artifact and as a narrative document, it stands alone among Anglo-Saxon artistic achievements. The poem remains an important text for English educators and is a standard of British literature courses throughout high schools in the United States. After all, where better to turn when we want to teach our students about the roots of English literature? Import and significance, however, do not a lesson plan make.

In this essay, I will discuss both the obstacles to students' reading and understanding *Beowulf* and the continuing allure that the poem may have for them. I will argue that, as a way to combat the obstacles but still capitalize on the allure, a blending of genres and a crossing of media are in order, namely in the form of the graphic novel. I will briefly detail some insufficient previous attempts to adapt *Beowulf* into graphic novel or comic book form and then argue that Gareth Hinds's most recent graphic novel adaptation (2000) not only preserves more of the poem than these previous attempts, but also handles the complexities of the story subtly, such that the end-product is artful and worthy of study in its own right. Moreover, Hinds's *Beowulf* suggests new ways for teachers and students to approach the poem, ways that will help the poem remain a vital work and an intriguing read for students.

Obstacles

Despite *Beowulf*'s traditional place in the English classroom, the poem presents real obstacles to reading—and therefore teaching. Foremost among these obstacles is the Old English language itself and the conventions of Old English poetic composition. Granted, nearly all students who read the poem in high school classrooms in the United States will do so in translation. Nevertheless, certain difficult or conspicuous elements linger, to which even sophisticated contemporary readers may not be accustomed. For example, to our modern ears, the Anglo-Saxon use of alliteration seems to be overdone. Phrases heavy with alliteration—such as "Then for the third time the people's foe, the fierce firedrake, was mindful on his feud" and "deprived many men of meadbenches"—draw attention to themselves, sound artificial, and therefore have the potential to distract a young reader.

Other elements, such as *Beowulf*'s vocabulary, its interlaced structure, its overtly Christian ideology, and even its length (weighing in at more than 3,000 lines), can be similarly discouraging, and these problems are sometimes compounded by translation as well. Although there are some dynamic modern translations (Burton Raffel's 1963 and Seamus Heaney's 1999 translations of *Beowulf* come to mind), they necessarily lose something of the original. What they gain in interest, they lose in accuracy. But more "literal," so-called word-for-word translations tend to be so flat or confounding that students lose interest and simply throw up their hands. Prose translations lose the poem's musical flow entirely. Recognizing these difficulties, teachers (and their standard anthologies) customarily choose to use excerpts from *Beowulf* for classroom use. Even though this technique certainly has its practicalities and merits, so much of the poem gets left behind that, I would argue, teaching in excerpts actually alters and corrupts the text. For instance, the most commonly anthologized excerpts are the three main "battle" scenes, in which Beowulf fights Grendel, Grendel's mother, and the dragon. But, in reality, these scenes account for relatively little of the poem.

Allure

The challenge for teachers is to combat these obstacles by taking advantage of what makes the poem attractive. Despite its many difficulties, it still appeals to many young readers for a variety of reasons. First, *Beowulf* is about, among other things, monsters. Vampires, werewolves, mummies, and a host of other scary creatures are, in many ways, the legacy of Grendel and his ilk. The trio of all-evil, villainous monsters in *Beowulf* rivals any contemporary horror flick, and the same attraction to ghost stories can lure even the most reticent readers to the poem.

Second, Beowulf as a character is a quintessential hero. The modern-day comic book superhero is heir to Beowulf's exploits and characteristics: strong, courageous, civic-minded, virtually infallible. The same attraction young people have to Spider-Man, Superman, and others of their kind operates here too. This attraction to monsters and heroes is by no means a contemporary phenomenon. As Walter Ong points out in *Orality and Literacy* (1982), the role of such exceedingly monstrous and heroic characters in oral narratives such as *Beowulf*

> is best . . . explained in terms of the needs of oral noetic [i.e., thinking] process. Oral memory works effectively with "heavy" characters, persons whose deeds are monumental, memorable, and commonly public. Thus the noetic economy of its nature generates outsize figures, that is, heroic figures, not for romantic reasons or reflectively didactic reasons but for much more basic reasons: to organize experience in some sort of permanently memorable form. (p. 70)

Although it is expressed in highly academic terms here, the concept of oral noetic economy is very much comprehensible to students. After all, we teach them techniques such as oral mnemonics all the time to help their memories in school. The use of "heavy" characters in Anglo-Saxon poetry is no more than a historically and culturally situated mnemonic device.

The third basis for the poem's continuing appeal, one intimately related to the first two, is that *Beowulf* is, to a great degree, a visually told narrative, often very graphic, and sometimes violently gruesome. The image of Grendel's ripped-off arm hanging from the rafters of Heorot is not dissimilar to the kind of graphic images young people may encounter in video games, on television, and in movies such as the *Star Wars* series, where the loss of an arm or hand happens so often as to become a symbolic theme. Oral narratives often portray physical violence because, as Ong points out, "Violence in oral art forms is also connected with the structure of orality itself. When all verbal communication must be by direct word of mouth, involved in the give-and-take dynamics of sound, interpersonal relations are kept high—both attractions and, even more, antagonisms" (1982, p. 45). The world of *Beowulf*, Ong says, is a very visual and "highly polarized, agonistic, oral world of good and evil, virtue and vice, villains and heroes" (p. 45).

Finally, although I have argued that the Old English language presents a barrier to reading the poem, the language difference is also interesting enough that many students are intrigued by it. After all, the various Anglo-Saxon terms for the human body ("bone-cage," "soul-house") and other such kennings are evocative, descriptive, poetic, and, in the end, also clear and appropriate, as well as excellent fodder for creative writing (try asking students to name everyday things in their lives the way the Anglo-Saxons did—by using poetic and practical compound nouns). Often, the very oddity of the language, which in some cases tends to obstruct understanding, may also initiate a certain curiosity that gets young readers interested in *Beowulf*. With all of these attractions—the monsters, the hero, the graphic storytelling, and the interesting language—the trick then becomes to help young readers to persevere in their reading of the poem once the initial luster wears off. It is here that graphic novel adaptations, Hinds's in particular, can be as handy to have nearby as the battling Geat himself.

Previous Adaptations

Previous comic book and graphic novel versions of the poem range from the mediocre to the laughable. Michael Uslan and Ricardo Villamonte's short-lived DC comic, *Beowulf: Dragon Slayer* series (1975–1976), for example, cannot even claim to have stayed true to chronology, despite claims by assistant editor Allan Asherman that "we're doing it the RIGHT way!" (n.p.). If the capital letters and exclamation point don't tip the reader off that this version quite possibly exemplifies the WRONG way (!), then the titles of individual issues of the comic certainly will: *The Curse of Castle Hrothgar*; *Beowulf Meets Dracula*; *The Slave Maid of Satan!*; *The Serpent of Satan!*; *The Minotaur!*. These obviously indefensible treatments are indeed consistent with Asherman's desire to present "REAL LIVE action and adventure stories!" that are "EXCITING!" and "fast-paced." And yet the idea that these comics might have some "specific educational value" and that "you'll be proud to bring [them] into your classroom and show to your teacher" seems a tad optimistic. After all, why don't we adapt all classics in such a fashion? Consider comics with titles such as Odysseus in Space, Gilgamesh Goes Bowling, Aeneas in the Lost City of Atlantis.

Beyond optimistic is Uslan's claim that "we'll be doing what we can to capture the flavor and spirit of the poem (including the use of alliteration, internal rhyme, and the kenning)." I wonder which of these three poetic devices (of which internal rhyme functions very little in Old English verse) Uslan had in mind when the comic book Beowulf addresses Satan in Hell: "All right, Satan—what lurks in your treacherous mind? Why do you lure me into this diseased den of iniquity? Why do you give Castle Hrothgar a blood-bath?" Perhaps "diseased den" and "blood-bath" are supposed to stand in for the elaborate alliterative meter of *Beowulf*. Uslan and Villamonte's version, though entertaining in its own right (if only for the kitsch value), glaringly illustrates how not to present a classic in comic book form, especially in the classroom. Perhaps these comics could be used to entertain the idea of having students create "sequel adventures" to the text, but otherwise they have little educational value.

Then there is Jerry Bingham's attempt (1984) to recreate the text in comic form, which paints a thoroughly romantic picture of Beowulf as the epic hero in a tone that sounds more like a movie trailer than a poem:

> Born of a legendary time, coming from a land where legends are born, he crossed a Northern sea to make a mark in the pages of history that would long endure after the seas had turned to rivers and the mountains to sand. He was of a noble breed. He was . . . BEOWULF. (n.p.)

It is easy enough to scoff at Bingham for taking such hyperbolic liberties with the text, but the spirit of the attempt at least tries to render a heroism that might attract contemporary comic book readers. Moreover, although he alters the texts in arguably unwarrantable ways, at least he remains faithful to its chronology and the main events in the poem. Still, even if young readers pay attention to this and get the "basics" of the *Beowulf* storyline (as if a story only consists of its sequence of events), is this worth so radically altering the poem? Perhaps so. Amy D. Graves, a teacher in a central Virginia high school, used the Bingham graphic novel to augment her students' reading of the text. Graves had students compare Bingham's renderings of Grendel to their own artistic interpretations of the beast, to great effect, for class discussion. However, Graves admits that she found the Bingham novel to be missing too much of the overall story to use it extensively in class (A. D. Graves, personal communication, June 1, 2005).

But Hinds's Sight Is 20/20

It is not my intention to berate thirty-year-old comics for their inaccuracies and fabrications or to disrespect Bingham's admirable attempt. I only mean to place Gareth Hinds's pedagogically valuable adaptation of *Beowulf* in stark contrast to the previous attempts to visualize the poem. Not only is Hinds's artwork striking by itself (described by one reviewer as "drop dead gorgeous"), but he also has rendered a comic that takes the poem seriously and is truly worthy of it.

Hinds chooses the 1910 Gummere translation to accompany his fresh and often gruesome images; he claims to like Gummere's version because, as he says on the opening page of his graphic novel, "it preserves the essential feeling of Old English verse, particularly in its meter and alliteration." Although Hinds certainly seems to have done his homework on many aspects of Old English culture, his choice of translation may have been motivated more by the expired copyright of the Gummere translation than by its fidelity to the poem. (See http:// www.fordham.edu/halsall/basis/beowulf.html for the entire Gummere translation.) Also, Gummere employs a misleading brand of "Ye Olde" English archaism (e.g., "o'er" and "lo") that has nothing to do with the Anglo-Saxon language whatsoever and everything to do with the conventions for translations of his time.

In the end, however, it matters very little which translation Hinds chooses, because his graphic handling of the story captures something of *Beowulf* that all written text, however imagistic, however vividly rendered, fails to communicate. Remarkably, for instance, out of the forty pages in Book I that recount the Grendel portion of the poem, only fifteen of them have written text at all—except for onomatopoeic "words" (see Figure 5.1) found within action-oriented frames (e.g., "SKUTCHLP," "GLK!" " "SHLUK," "SMASH," etc.).

This leaning on visual storytelling is, in itself, one way that Hinds combats the major obstacle of the original text for student readers of *Beowulf*—its language. Although Hinds includes a glossary of unfamiliar words and definitions at the beginning of the book (e.g., "Thanes," "Scyldings"), soon enough the images become primary and the text takes a back seat, which, I would argue, may not be a bad thing so long as the poem itself is not replaced by, but rather taught in conjunction with, the graphic novel.

None of this is to suggest that Hinds's work surpasses the poem itself. His graphic novel stands in a long line of imaginative adaptations of *Beowulf*, some faithful and some not so faithful. His version, however, seems most useful pedagogically. Not only does it lighten some of the "load" of the text, but the comic also helps fill in gaps of knowledge for students about the aristocratic warrior culture that the poem portrays. Most students have preconceived ideas of what is "medieval," and they tend to equate the Dark Ages with the castles and knights in shining armor of the chivalric period, when, in fact, a text that naturally follows chronologically might actually be something Arthurian. For example, students might be asked to consider the difference between the heroic code expressed in *Beowulf* and the chivalric code of King Arthur's knights. But Hinds paints a darker and, finally, more accurate picture of the North. For instance, he shows a Heorot (see Figure 5.2) constructed of wood, which is archaeologically more accurate, whereas other comic book versions (e.g., Bingham's and Uslan and Villamonte's) depict a stone fortress.

Figure 5.1. Hinds's effective use of onomatopoeia.

Figure 5.2. A Hinds illustration that provides some historically accurate detail.

This is only one example, and an investigation of the archaeology of *Beowulf* may abet students' interest in the history of some of the items in the poem, such as swords, helmets, and shields. Teachers may even try developing webquests to help students find images of such items and have them compare their findings to the graphic novel to test Hinds's interpretations (a list of possible links is provided at the end of this chapter).

Educators have become increasingly aware of the importance of different learning styles; it is clear that comics and graphic novels can be effective tools for reaching visual learners. Also, comics are an ideal medium to spark further interests in students, who then learn to equate reading with enjoyment, thus beginning the development of a reading habit. But teachers should be very explicit about the texts they choose to use in the classroom and explain clearly that the graphic novel *Beowulf* is an adaptation and therefore a complement to the poem rather than a substitution. Although others might differ, in no way do I argue that the graphic novel should be preferred over the text itself. After all, without the original poem itself, there would be no sequential art adaptation. Once this is established, the poem's themes present a productive place for teachers to begin discussing the poem and the graphic novel in conjunction with it.

Hero

Because heroism is a concept everyone is familiar with, it is a good theme to start with in a classroom discussion. There are so many different kinds of heroism that students may find it easy to connect Beowulf with other literary or popular culture heroes they already know about. Also, because the graphic novel supplies them with an actual image of the hero (see Figure 5.3), good questions to ask are the following (with "answers" to aid teachers and help prompt further class discussion or debate):

- *Why is Beowulf painted as he is?*
  Beowulf initially appears to be a good, noble leader who has come to help Hrothgar. He stands at the prow of his ship with a beatific half-smile on his face. Although he is nearly a head taller than everyone else, it is not until he removes his clothing that we see he is also as muscular and brawny as any of today's professional wrestlers. This tension between being a leader and a warrior is at the heart of both the poem and the graphic novel. The artist may be trying to provide clues to this via his representation of the Geat warrior.

Figure 5.3. Beowulf fighting Grendel.

- *What does he look like in the beginning as opposed to the ending? What do you think is the significance of this?*
  At the beginning of the graphic novel, the young Beowulf is often shown with his head bowed, showing deference to Hrothgar, in whose hall, Heorot, he is a guest. At the end of the graphic novel, Beowulf is now King of the Geats, having ruled wisely for fifty years. Although he is still depicted as physically much larger than those around him, Beowulf seems to droop, struggling even to seat himself on his throne, a world-weary king who hangs his head now, not in deference but in sadness at the havoc the dragon has wreaked on his people.

- *What is a king or a hero supposed to look like?*
  The beauty of Hinds's portrayal of Beowulf is his use of the traditional physical characteristics of the hero. The hero is bigger than everyone else but respectful. He is decisive but not rash. He is the center of each panel he appears in, but his deeds are done to help others. He rejoices in his victory over the monsters, but he does not dwell on his achievements, accepting his laurels humbly. Beowulf's appearance as king, however, differs markedly from that of the stereotypical hero. Whereas before he was the plain-dressed hero, now he is the decorated and bejeweled king. But when he decides to fight the dragon, Hinds strips him down to a more basic image of the hero.

- *If he is a hero, why does Beowulf die at the end?*
  Beowulf dies in the end because he must. His heroic life is portrayed as a series of great feats of courage and strength. As a now enfeebled king, though still remarkably powerful by ordinary standards, he must protect his people against the ravages of the dragon. He does this by sacrificing himself. Critics have argued over the melancholic tone of the poem's end, and there is by no means a standard interpretation. Ultimately, however, the poem can be read as an exultation, despite fate, of a hero-king's extraordinary life and accomplishments, tinged with an inspiring sadness.

- *What is the difference between Beowulf and Superman (or some other readily recognizable hero)?*
  Although many similarities can be found between Beowulf and modern superheroes—the desire to protect the innocent, supernatural powers, the esteem of others—the differences are sometimes more illuminating. For one, part of the heroic ethos of Beowulf would be defined by the need to boast. Unferth's taunting of Beowulf, artfully and somewhat comically rendered by Hinds, illustrates this kind of Anglo-Saxon verbal contest. Second, unlike his modern counterparts, Beowulf is not just a protector of people; indeed, he is also their leader. Finally, and partially related to the first two differences, Beowulf's identity, which is so vital to his heroism, is not unknown or kept hidden.

The theme of the hero provides opportunities for a discussion of courage, selflessness, and other defining characteristics. Students can also try to answer the question of whether they think Beowulf is the same hero in the comic that he is in the poem: that is, does painting a picture of him actually change him?

Monster

In much the same way that students develop the idea of heroism, they can develop and discuss the image of the monster:

- *What makes something or someone monstrous?*
  The three monsters in Beowulf have specific characteristics that define them as monstrous beyond their supernatural powers or superhuman strengths. Grendel is unreasonable, chaotic, and perversely violent. Grendel's mother is temperamental and vengeful. The dragon is vengeful too, as well as excessively greedy. Moreover, each one of these monsters, like many monsters, is feared because he or she is not human and therefore has no sense of human morality.

- *What is the difference, if any, between a monster and a villain?*
  Unlike monsters, villains are subject to human and natural laws. Villains are villainous precisely because they are humans that, in some way or other, attempt to transgress these laws. Whereas villains are considered sociopaths, we don't expect monsters to behave well.

- *In Beowulf, which of the monsters is the most vividly imagined in the graphic novel? In the poem?*
  Hinds's treatments of all three monsters are vivid, each one in its own way, but Grendel comes across as the most distinct. He is a bulky black image against the various brown colors of Heorot. His mother, on the other hand, is always shown monochromatically—a deep blue underwater, a reddish-brown in her den. And the dragon almost melts into the blacks and grays of the final section. This treatment makes sense when compared with the poem, in which Grendel is also given a more detailed description. After all, he is the only one of the trio of monsters with a name of his own.

- *Which one seems to be the most dangerous monster or the scariest? Why?*
  The answer to this question depends on what the individual reader is most afraid of. On one hand, because Grendel represents a chaotic and irrational force, a person who tends to be afraid of losing control of situations may consider him to be the scariest. But because the dragon is so large and has the ability to wreak havoc on an entire people, a person who values com-

munity may find it to be the most frightful. The important element in this question is to ask why a monster may evoke certain feelings. A more invested reading will allow the reader to
make personal contact with a poem that may otherwise resist
such identification.

- *Is there a difference between the graphic novel and the poem in the
  levels or kinds of monstrosity?*
  The main difference between the graphic novel and the poem
  in the level of monstrosity is the explicit and graphic presentation of the monster's ravages. For instance, where the poem
  describes Grendel's mother as snatching Hrothgar's advisor,
  Æschere, from his bed, the graphic novel shows her long, sharp
  claws hovering over his face; a turn of the page reveals Æschere's
  bloodied head amid a writhing mound of snakes. On the whole,
  however, the difference in monstrosity is not in kind, but in
  degree. In this way, Hinds stays true to the poem while taking
  advantage of the graphic novel medium.

Comparisons between *Beowulf*'s monsters and other literary monsters
(such as *Frankenstein's*) would make for productive class discussion as
well. Who "created" Grendel? Why is he ravaging Heorot? This line of
questioning, interestingly enough, could even lead to a discussion of
Christianity in the poem.

Christianity

In order to present the context of the poem clearly to students, it is important to dwell, at least briefly, on the poem's Christian perspective.
Directing students to the graphic novel version of *Beowulf* in order to
find Christian elements has the danger of lapsing into an enjoyable but
limited game of seek-and-find, so teachers may want to emphasize that
the poem itself is considered to be fundamentally, unapologetically
Christian. Students may be able to take a critical step further and compare the narrator's announcement of Christian motifs to Hinds's sometimes subtle strategies of weaving Christian images into the graphic
novel. For example, Grendel is introduced in the poem as a "fiend from
hell" (p. 101), "Cain's kin" (p. 107); later the poet says that Grendel "bore
God's wrath" (p. 711), an artful double meaning suggesting that the
"wicked ravager" is intended to be both the one who is punished for
his evil nature and the punisher of Heorot. But Hinds does not rely on
the poem's text to communicate these Christian elements. Rather, his
images do the work. Beowulf is shown numerous times as a meek,
Christ-like figure, with his arms outstretched in the shape of a cross.
Later, however, he emerges from the den of Grendel's mother holding

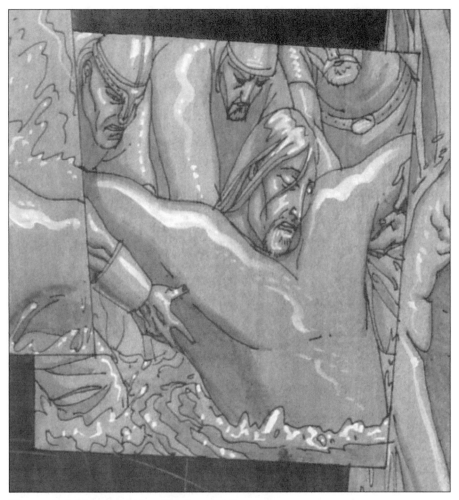

Figure 5.4. Beowulf being lifted out of the water.

the cross-shaped hilt of the magical sword he found there, looking now like a grotesque and bloodied warrior of the cross. A turn of the page shows a slumping, exhausted Beowulf helped from the water (see Figure 5.4), appearing, once again, both meek and Christ-like. Moreover, in class discussions it may be meaningful for teachers to inquire into the ideas of crime and punishment in a Christian context. Is Grendel God's punishment? Is Beowulf God's mercy? Teachers may be reluctant to pursue such questions in detail in public schools but still need to keep in mind that the poem's religious context is inseparable from its literary and historical context. Nevertheless, discussion of Christianity in *Beowulf* need not turn into a theological debate.

Visual Form

Hinds's artistic decisions also make for excellent discussion among classroom participants. "What is the function of Hinds's color palette?" a teacher might ask. After all, the first book is in browns, the second in blues and greens, and the third in black and white. In an interview entitled "Classics Redrawn" in July 2000, Hinds said of the color (and textural) differences among the three parts of his *Beowulf,* "Obviously, there's this sort of parchment-wood-stone progression . . . , and I don't know exactly what it means, but the point is that it evokes something that's appropriate to the story." Teachers might pose the following questions: What is it exactly that Hinds cannot seem to describe in words but feels to be true to the story? What is the "something that's appropriate to the story?" Another avenue of critical discussion might be to talk about Hinds's use of sometimes jagged, sometimes slanted panel borders rather than straight right-to-left and up-and-down lines. Here, teachers might ask: When does Hinds use slanted borders? When does he choose not to? Why? Hinds has said that he "tend[s] to keep text to a minimum" in his work. Students may have reactions to the question: What is the result of this emphasis on image?

Structure

Beowulf's three battles constitute only about 15 percent of the entire poem, and yet these scenes are the ones most lovingly and lengthily rendered in the comic. It is boasting, rejoicing, congratulating, advising, and other kinds of speaking—rather than fighting—that actually take up the greater portion of *Beowulf* the poem. Today, however, few serious storytellers—including television producers, filmmakers, comic book artists, etc.—focus on this kind of speaking or include such scenes in their narratives, although it is the case that rap music and many forms of informal student speech mirror this language. Indeed, having students think about popular culture counterparts to these speaking patterns might prove fruitful. Along these same lines, class discussions might consider these questions: Would Beowulf's peers consider him to be "The Man"? Would his soldiers "do the dozens" with each other or with their enemies and make beots (boasts) to amplify their brawn and prowess? What song reminds students most of the sometimes boastful tenor of these characters? If the story of Beowulf were set to a rap tune, what would the lyrics be like? Things have to be happening constantly to hold on to a reader's attention, and since readers of comic book narratives may focus on their visual literacy to appreciate the story fully, linguistic interplays might seem tedious to some students. Hinds understands this principle. By both blending and eliding the passage of time, he is able to suggest the verbal scenes of *Beowulf* without actually having to slow down the story. It is important here to note that, unlike the original poem or its modern translations, in which the basic unit of written text is the line, Hinds's creation is able to manipulate time this way because the basic unit of the graphic novel is the panel. On the page, not only can Hinds make the past coexist with the present by simply having the two images placed next to each other, but the borders between panels and the turning of the page itself also simulate the forward movement of time. Different media present different possibilities whose capabilities and limitations can be examined in the classroom.

Also, what are the differences between hearing a story told, reading a story, and seeing a story? Film comparisons are familiar to students, and, in many ways, the comic book can be discussed as a medium between a text and a film. Moreover, although the difference between orality and literacy is a question that linguists and language philosophers still wrestle with, it is in no way over the heads of young readers. Teachers could begin with the idea that stories composed orally differ in fundamental ways from stories composed in writing, mainly in their formulaic arrangement. Thought and expression in oral cultures tend to be heavily formulaic. As in Homer's *Iliad* and *Odyssey*, *Beowulf* is made up "not simply of word units, but of formulas" (Ong, 1982, p. 58) that are crucial elements of the diction and syntax of the poem. Classroom discussions of the differences between these more traditional modes of narration, along with the question of visual narrative, may be fruitful. Living in an unabashedly visual culture, young readers are, in many ways, better equipped than their teachers in terms of a critically insightful visual literacy.

Beowulf's interlaced structure, which is a literary counterpoint to the Dark Ages' decorative arts, can be difficult for a young reader to grapple with. Fortunately, there are decorative illustrations of interlacing in Hinds's graphic novel. And, by making a point of talking about interlacing (the digressions, multiple narratives, assumed knowledge, etc.), teachers may be able to dispel confusions preemptively. A good question to ask of the graphic novel is the following: How are the digressions and asides handled? The intertwining of past and present is literal in the comic, but in the text the pattern has to be teased out, which can be tedious or confusing. Modern notions of "flashback" in both literature and film are appropriate discussion points. The analysis can go beyond that, however, and explore the intricacy and complexity of the interlaced patterns. Concerning interlacing, teachers might ask these questions: What kind of knowledge is taken for granted in *Beowulf*?

What kind of knowledge is taken for granted in stories of today? The interlacing is sometimes overlooked by both students and teachers because the three most commonly used excerpts of *Beowulf* are generally composed of brief highlights of the straightforward, linear narrative portions of the poem. But the interlaced pattern of the original poem offers a number of surprisingly interesting points of departure for good classroom discussion.

Writing Strategies

A teacher can assign a number of different kinds of writing exercises in conjunction with the reading of both the poem and the comic. Creative responses to each text may include filling in the fifty-year gap of time between the killing of Grendel's mother and the slaying of the dragon. Or students may write from the point of view of a character other than Beowulf. The authoritative narrator of the poem offers his own commentary, so a student might imagine the narrator or storyteller as a character. Critical writing assignments could tackle the themes of Christianity, oral and visual storytelling, or heroism and courage.

Students could also go online to view Hinds's website (http://www.thecomic.com), where there are a number of his other comics, some adaptations, and other original stories. This online activity could be used as a springboard to writing about the choices that authors make when adapting older works. Also to be found online is the previously mentioned interview with Gareth Hinds, in which he talks about some of these choices in adaptation. For instance, he says in the "Classics Redrawn" interview, "I essentially wanted to do a superhero book, without the modern superhero conventions." A writing assignment might include a critical exploration of how the conceptions of literary heroism and superheroism have either changed or have stayed the same through time. In response to the questions "What do you think *Beowulf* gains by keeping the traditional approach?" and "What do you think *Beowulf* loses by not taking a more modern approach to storytelling?," Hinds says,

> I'd say I sacrifice a degree of literal believability in order to preserve or enhance the mythological weight of the story (I'm not sure I would agree that one is traditional and one modern). . . . Sacrifice may not be a good word, though, because I think both elements are preserved . . . when you read *Beowulf* you are aware that there is a human drama going on (I think). It's just a question of what the author chooses to explicitly meditate on. (n.p.)

A fruitful writing assignment might be to consider what, if anything, Hinds sacrifices in his handling of *Beowulf* and to answer the following question: Is the reader aware that a human drama is going on?

Post-Reading Activities

The natural post-reading exercise is to have students create their own *Beowulf* comic. But rather than having them simply mimic Hinds, it should be emphasized that their personal image of the narrative should be somehow different. The graphic novel and the poem should both be considered as points of departure for their own versions. In fact, a good starting point would be to encourage students to select scenes from the poem that Hinds chose to leave out. In this way, a critical discussion may arise as to why Hinds included the scenes he did. Also, experimenting with adaptation is both an aesthetic exercise and a means to foster critical thinking. Students might be assigned in groups to invent their own Old English hero-king or queen, and, if they are so inclined, they can even draw their own comic book version.

Conclusions

In teaching *Beowulf* and its comic book adaptation, we accomplish the dual task of teaching literature and that of promoting and fostering critical thinking and learning through visual literacy. There is a commonly held prejudice that images are only used to help young and inexperienced readers with the printed word. For example, as Karen Day (1996) puts it, pictures in books are for "little kids" and are "to be put aside when young readers 'really' read" (p. 69). But this attitude does not take into account that the combination of visual and verbal elements allows the reader to make "critical interpretations of greater significance than would be possible if visual and verbal texts were read as separate elements" (p. 74). Most likely, the verbal text enjoys this privilege because of the primacy of visual literacy, which is thought of as an early stage that a student should grow out of. Revising these notions permits us to consider visual literacy not so much as a phase, but rather as a foundation for all subsequent experience. But as Richard Sinatra argues in *Visual Literacy Connections to Thinking, Reading, and Writing* (1986), "The basic structure of thought enumerates from a non-verbal core and forms the basis of symbolic thinking, classification, and reversibility of thought" (p. 8).

 Beowulf will continue to be taught in high schools. We all recognize its value, but as teachers we must find ways to live up to the quality of the poem—not because reading old texts is "good for us," but because, as Gareth Hinds recognizes, they are often artfully told and compelling stories. Modern adaptors of ancient stories have the challenge not only of dealing with aesthetic and practical considerations, but also of reminding us that these stories are worth retelling in the first place.

Some *Beowulf*-Related Links

Ralph Bucci's *Beowulf* webquest: http://falconlit.com/web/webquest/beowulf/

"Hero Journey" and "Nature of Evil" webquests: http://www.polytechnic.org/faculty/lholmgren

General *Beowulf* resources: http://www.georgetown.edu/faculty/irvinem/english016/beowulf/beowulf.html

http://www.uky.edu/~kiernan/eBeowulf/guide.htm

http://www.a2armory.com/ (commercial site)

http://www.ece.northwestern.edu/~pred/medieval/

http://labyrinth.georgetown.edu/

http://www.humanities.mcmaster.ca/~beowulf/archeology.html

Excellent site for Anglo-Saxon armor: http://spider.georgetown college.edu/english/allen/helmets.htm

References

Bingham, J. (1984). *Beowulf.* Evanston, IL: First Comics.

Day, K. (1996). From the eighteenth-century illustrated book to contemporary children's picture books: Teaching the "third text." In W. F. Garrett-Petts and D. Lawrence (Eds.), *Integrating visual and verbal literacies* (pp. 69–75). Winnipeg, Canada: Inkshed Publications.

Hinds, G. (2000). *The Collected Beowulf.* Cambridge, MA: THECOMIC.COM.

Hinds, G. (2000). Interview by Karon Flage: Classics redrawn. Retrieved August 1, 2004, from http://www.sequentialart.com/archive/july00/hinds.shtml

Ong, W. (1982). *Orality and literacy: The technologizing of the word.* New York: Methuen.

Sinatra, R. (1986). *Visual literacy connections to thinking, reading, and writing.* Springfield, IL: C. C. Thomas.

Uslan, M., & Villamonte, R. (1975). *Beowulf: Dragon slayer.* New York: DC Comics.

6 L. Frank Baum, Lewis Carroll, James Barrie, and *Pop Gun War:* Teaching Farel Dalrymple's Graphic Novel in the Context of Classics

Randall Clark
Clayton State University

Introduction

The story of a boy who acquires wings and the ability to fly, *Pop Gun War* (2003), Farel Dalrymple's graphic novel, is part of a well-established subgenre of fantasy literature, one in which young protagonists try to function within a surreal world that is radically different from the life that we all recognize. Some of these works, such as C. S. Lewis's *Chronicles of Narnia*, are overtly didactic, presenting their moral lessons clearly and obviously. Others are meant to be taken as grand adventures with an element of social commentary. *Pop Gun War* falls into the latter category and, in particular, bears a resemblance to many established classics of young adult literature such as James Barrie's *Peter Pan*, Lewis Carroll's *Alice in Wonderland* and *Through the Looking Glass*, and L. Frank Baum's *Wizard of Oz* (originally titled *The Wonderful Wizard of Oz*) and his other novels about Oz. Dalrymple's work differs from that of Barrie, Carroll, and Baum in a significant manner, however. Although their protagonists are typically children who travel from their own societies to other, more fanciful worlds, in *Pop Gun War* the focus is on a boy whose surreal adventures take place in his own hometown, a bizarre variation of an American metropolis. By highlighting a child's attempt to make sense of his native culture, *Pop Gun War* offers a theme that has not been explored in these other novels and thus serves as an interesting complement. Also, unlike the other works, *Pop Gun War* has received little critical attention to date and is just now starting to make its way out of the "comics world" and into the realm of young adult literature. This essay examines the major themes and influences of Dalrymple's work such that someone hearing about it for the first time can gain a strong understanding of its critical and pedagogical value. Primarily, the graphic novel will be explored in relation to the three classics already mentioned and with respect to how the texts might be used together. But other teaching ideas are also presented, as connections to other common readings for middle and high school students emerge from the analysis of Dalrymple's work, which is rich in literary allusions.

Pop Gun War as a Literary Reference or Review

Like many contemporary authors, Dalrymple is quite willing to acknowledge his influences; he tends to give tribute by his use of place names and names of characters. Teachers can take advantage of this habit by using his graphic novel as an engaging "literary review" for their most astute and skilled students or by pairing the novel with any number of other texts. For example, inside the front cover and on the first page of *Pop Gun War*, a detailed map is included of an urban setting area known only as "The City." Dalrymple's protagonist is named Sinclair, like the first name of one great American novelist, Sinclair Lewis, and the surname of another, Upton Sinclair. Melville Bridge must be named for the author of *Moby-Dick*; in fact, one of the characters in *Pop Gun War* quotes from that novel directly. (Another quotes the Scottish poet Robert Burns; it seems that the residents of The City are unusually literate.) Likewise, Karamazov Castle is surely an allusion to *The Brothers Karamazov*. Nemo's Village could refer to characters from two different fantasies: Captain Nemo of Jules Verne's *Twenty Thousand Leagues under the Sea* or Little Nemo, of the early twentieth-century Winsor McCay comic strip (given the similarities between cartoonist McCay's artwork and Dalrymple's, the latter seems more likely). Other artists are referred to as well. Dr. Wyeth may well be a tribute to the American painter Andrew Wyeth, and Flagg Beach could be named after the great illustrator James Montgomery Flagg. And despite any overt reference to Orson Welles's films, it can't be a coincidence that The City has both an Orson Airstrip and a Welles River. There are also allusions to the Bible—places named Golgoth and Gehenna—and to the history of the French Revolution—Lake Robespierre.

Bonus Teaching Idea

Teachers may explore any or all of these guiding questions as the class explores the graphic novel: Are there parallels between The City and meatpacking Chicago? Is there an element of muckraking to Dalrymple's style or characters? What is the significance of quoting directly from Moby-Dick*? From Robert Burns? Why does Dalrymple name places in his graphic novel Golgoth and Gehenna?*

Back to Baum, Carroll, and Barrie

Despite the many references to other works, it is Baum, Carroll, and Barrie who most immediately influence *Pop Gun War* in setting, character, and narrative. *Pop Gun War's* premise—that a child could find wings discarded by an angel, place them on his own back, fly, and then grow a new set of wings after losing the ones he had found—is fantastic, yet it is logical within the confines of the novel. If wings exist, why shouldn't they be transferable, something one could wear as a hand-me-down, like an article of clothing? The novel's whimsical fantasy, predicated on a contorted version of the real world, places it in the same domain as *The Wizard of Oz*, *Peter Pan*, and *Alice in Wonderland*. After all, F. Baum makes it seem perfectly reasonable that the body of a flesh-and-blood man could be gradually replaced by tin after a series of accidents. Barrie maintains that a fairy should be born whenever a baby laughs for the first time and die whenever a disbelief in fairies is expressed. Carroll finds it natural that one could play croquet with flamingos. Furthermore, Dalrymple shares more than just a sense of whimsy with *Peter Pan*, the Oz novels, and the Alice stories: their influence on *Pop Gun War* is clear. Dalrymple reuses some of their noteworthy elements: the child protagonist who remains childlike, non sequitur dialogue, the absent parent, a symbolic escape from the real world, anthropomorphism, characters who change in impossible ways, and occurrences that are illogical despite the internal logic of the narrative. Teachers might consider exploring these elements with their students by using the four works in a literary unit built around the theme of "fantasy worlds" or "fantastical bildungsromans."

Wings and Flight

Pop Gun War begins when an angel, later shown to be the angel of death, crashes to Earth, where he pays a construction worker to remove his wings with a chainsaw. The juxtaposition of realistic setting and fantasy exhibited in this opening scene remains an important element of the novel. Sinclair, an African American boy, finds the discarded wings in a trash can, takes them home, and straps them on. The passage of the wings from the angel to Sinclair is reminiscent of Dorothy's obtaining the silver slippers (ruby slippers were a Hollywood invention) from the dead witch in *The Wizard of Oz*. Like the wings, the slippers bring with them a certain amount of power and ability, and, like Dorothy, Sinclair faces challenges to his ownership of this mystic acquisition. But this scene also has parallels in *Peter Pan*: the Darling children have seen Peter in their dreams but are only able to meet him after he leaves a part of himself, his shadow, in their bedroom.

The *Peter Pan* comparison is strengthened by the fact that the wings allow Sinclair to fly, just as Wendy and her brothers are taught to fly by Peter. The difference is in the way that the children learn that they can fly. In *Peter Pan*, "no one can fly unless the fairy dust has been blown on him." Peter blows dust on the Darlings "with the most superb results. 'Now just wriggle your shoulders this way,' he said, 'and let go'" (Barrie, 1987, p. 37). The Darlings then fly happily to Neverland. In comparison, Sinclair learns to fly after he tries to stop a group of boys from beating up a homeless man named Addison who is sleeping in an alley. The boys turn on Sinclair, chase him to the top of a building, and throw rocks at him. It is only when one of the rocks knocks him off the building that Sinclair realizes that he can fly. The Darlings's ability is depicted as a product of belief, but Sinclair's flight is the product of necessity.

Having wings complicates Sinclair's life. In an inversion of Dorothy, Alice, and the Darlings, he is not a normal person surrounded by strange beings; rather, it is Sinclair who has become abnormal. When he attempts to fit in with the normal residents of The City, he fails. Coming upon a group of his friends playing ball, Sinclair attempts to join in, but the game quickly breaks up as the police arrive. When the boys congregate again in an alley, Sinclair points out that they'd done nothing wrong and shouldn't have run away. Of course, in the real world, arrests can be made even more capriciously than in Wonderland, so the boys think they did the right thing by fleeing. "You don't know anything," one boy tells Sinclair. "You think you're so smart. Leave us alone" (Dalrymple, 2003, p. 46). Another boy even blames Sinclair for the game's breaking up: "We were having fun. Why did you have to ruin it?" (p. 47). Significantly, the other boys don't even comment on the fact that Sinclair now has wings and is in fact hovering above ground during this entire conversation; it apparently goes without saying that he's at fault just because he's different.

Sinclair also has to face accusations that he stole the wings (Figure 6.1). He finds Addison standing on the street arguing with Mr. Koole, a man who once stole children's toys but has reformed, at least temporarily. A third party, R. K., is present as well, but, although he appears to be human, there is something unnatural about him—only Sinclair can see him and he has the ability to control Addison and Koole to a degree. Like Mephistopheles, R. K. tempts others to do evil; first he accuses Sinclair of stealing the wings and then he gets Koole to accuse him as well. Earlier in the novel, Addison, who is presumably stronger of character, has shown that he can resist this strange R. K. being to some degree. Sinclair's response to these accusations is significant; first he states, correctly, that he found the wings, but then he quickly changes his story, saying, "They were a gift" (Dalrymple, 2003, p. 42), as if the wings had been passed on to him by a higher power. Koole later confronts Sinclair and snatches his wings off, but the wings grow back, proving that Sinclair rightfully owns them, or, as Sinclair puts it, "They really were a gift" (p. 55).

Bonus Teaching Idea

Those not interested in pairing Pop Gun War *with other novel-length works might consider teaching it with an appropriate short story—Gabriel García Márquez's "A Very Old Man with Enormous Wings." Another similarly themed text is found in the lyrics to Pearl Jam's song "Given to Fly." In each example, wings bring trouble for the characters, and both texts deal with suspension of disbelief in intriguing ways.*

Temptation as Theme: The Influence of Evil

An equally Mephistophelian character, Mr. Grimshaw, enters the novel soon thereafter. Grimshaw is first seen interviewing Sinclair's sister, Emily, a musician and lead singer of her band, The Emilies. He later shows up at one of The Emilies's concerts, admitting that he is not really a journalist but is actually "a representative for a magnificent cor-

Figure 6.1. Sinclair's wings cause him problems.

poration." Like a certain character in Marlowe's *Doctor Faustus*, Grimshaw offers the band a contract, which they decline. Grimshaw tells them, "You will sell yourselves to someone. Probably in such small ways you might not realize it is happening" (Dalrymple, 2003, p. 65). He is less direct than Mephistopheles. Or is this in fact a warning, such as Mephistopheles offers the good doctor? We then see Addison having a dream that could either explain his past (but are dreams credible?) or be a foretelling of his future. In the dream, Addison also has dealings with Grimshaw, who elevates him from a homeless, unemployed person to a renowned artist. The mysterious R. K. is also present to plant a seed of doubt in Addison's mind about the quality of the art. Eventually, Addison does what The Emilies will not do: he sells out, placing money over art and rationalizing his decision by saying that he has a family to support.

Grimshaw and R. K. likely have more to do with *Faust* or *Doctor Faustus* than with *Alice in Wonderland*, *Peter Pan*, or *The Wizard of Oz*, but it should be noted that the children in those books also face temptation, particularly The Darlings, who could remain in Neverland forever if they fail to make a conscious effort to resist the charms of eternal youth and return home. The theme of temptation is one worth exploring with students regardless of which works are discussed along with *Pop Gun War*.

Grimshaw also comes into conflict with another character, Sunshine Montana, who is devoted to his pet, Percy, a huge fish who wears glasses and lives out of water (he is literally the "fish out of water" in a novel that has, figuratively, many such characters). Sunshine is the only person other than Sinclair who can see R. K., who calls him by the nickname "Sunny"; Sunshine also converses with the fallen angel and apparently sees no contradiction in being friendly with both. Sunshine is a dwarf, and, speaking before a crowd of young men, he suddenly begins to grow. "Your interest has made me grow," he tells the crowd. But the crowd is not interested in him at all, but flocking to see Grimshaw, who has, in a bag, a talking head that encourages the young men to misbehave, smoke cigarettes, throw trash on the streets, and not think too much. The boys abandon Sunshine, with one of them explaining "You were fun to watch when you were little, but now . . . He's got a head in a bag. That's neat" (Dalrymple, 2003, p. 79). Sunshine vows to keep growing and eventually reaches giant size. Changing size is a theme in *Alice in Wonderland* as well. But Alice had to eat from the mushroom to grow so dramatically, even though all that was required for Sunshine was sheer force of will. Grimshaw eventually loses control of the talking head after being attacked by two men who are possibly under the influence of R. K. The head is then found by the angel and placed in a trash can. Grimshaw recovers and entices all of the children in The City, with the sole exception of Sinclair, to come to The Doll Factory to see a puppet show.

Again, these sequences suggest a rich context of literary antecedents in addition to *The Wizard of Oz*, *Alice in Wonderland*, and *Peter Pan*. The concept of luring away an entire city of children is easily recognized as coming from the fairy tale "The Pied Piper of Hamlin." The gathering of boys who are easily led to misbehave is reminiscent of *Pinocchio*. But there are also connections here to Baum, Carroll, and Barrie. The boys that are led away might be a variation on *Peter Pan*'s lost boys. In one of his more obvious attempts at satire, Barrie says that the lost boys are unclaimed children who have fallen out of their baby carriages: "If they are not claimed in seven days they are sent far away to the Neverland to defray expenses" (Barrie, 1987, p. 31). The boys of *Pop Gun War*, growing up in the lower income neighborhood of The City, have also been neglected as a means of "defraying expenses." The imperious talking head in a box has much in common with the queen from *Alice in Wonderland*. Indeed, the passage culminates in a specific reference to *The Wizard of Oz* (see Figure 6.2).

Following directions from Percy, Sinclair tracks the missing children to The Doll Factory. The puppet show has ended, but Grimshaw refuses to let the children leave. "I miss my mom," says one child, echoing a common complaint of the Darlings in *Peter Pan*. Sinclair confronts Grimshaw and knocks his hat off, revealing him to be a robot. "I read *The Wizard of Oz*," Sinclair says. "I know how this works" (Dalrymple, 2003, p. 124). He pulls back a curtain to reveal a meek puppeteer, Harold Dollpimple—Dalrymple has taken Baum's concept one step further and named his own "wizard" after himself. Like the wizard, Dollpimple was motivated by good intentions—he wanted to place the children under his protection, where they would be safe from the violence in The City— but his plans got out of control. Dollpimple is also a worse person at heart than Oz's wizard; he is a megalomaniac, who is susceptible to the urgings of R. K. There is a hint that the evil may return. For now, however, Sinclair is happy, and things are largely good in The City. The angel allows Sinclair to keep his wings; in exchange, he rides Sinclair's bike into the heavens. Addison agrees to take a greater interest in his own life. Sinclair flies again. For now, temptation and evil are kept at bay.

Figure 6.2. A scene from *Pop Gun War* that resonates with allusions to *The Wizard of Oz*.

Setting and The City

In addition to drawing heavily on the works of Barrie, Baum, and Carroll for his narrative, Dalrymple also makes use of these works in the setting of his novel. Of course, in order to compare The City in *Pop Gun War* to Neverland, Wonderland, and Oz, teachers and students must be familiar with those other fantasy worlds. Unfortunately, as a result of familiarity with the various adaptations of these classics, some of the most important elements of the original novels may need to be reviewed: students sometimes forget, for example, that Oz is not the product of Dorothy's dream, but a physical place that she returns to multiple times and that her cousin also visits. Similarly forgotten but explicitly stated by Barrie, there are many Neverlands, each the product of a child's imagination. In other words, Neverland is what many believe Oz to be, a fantasy world unique to the individual. The only reason that all three Darlings are able to go to the same Neverland is due to an overlap in their imagined worlds, partly because they are siblings. Since Wonderland exists only as Alice's dream, it too can be viewed as an individual fantasy. Teachers need to help students make these critical, interesting, but complex distinctions, especially since inaccuracies from movie adaptations are so engrained in the popular culture.

Significantly, Dalrymple has borrowed characteristics of both the individual fantasy and the self-sufficient fantasy world. Because he has created a complement to the earlier works, rather than an imitation of them, The City in *Pop Gun War* serves as a fusion of the personal dream existence of Neverland and Wonderland and the separate and independent existence of Oz. *Pop Gun War* functions within the boundaries of both.

Bonus Teaching Idea

For those seeking shorter works to pair with Pop Gun War, *Hawthorne's short story "Wakefield" offers an interesting view on city life and shares with the graphic novel a certain interplay of visual and psychological elements.*

Although The City is not a product of Sinclair's imagination, the story told in *Pop Gun War* does read like a boy's dream, with the boy himself as hero: Sinclair is able to fly, proves himself smarter than adults, is referred to by Sunshine as "Young Master," and saves the day when he alone recognizes that Grimshaw is actually a robot. Having a sibling who is a rock singer would be very appealing to a younger boy, as opposed to a teenager who would probably rather fantasize about being a rock star himself. Even the possibly telepathic fish might seem pretty cool to a child. On the other hand, although he achieves a certain measure of wish fulfillment, there is ample evidence that Sinclair has no real power over the world in which he lives. His first words in the novel, "I'm not old enough," are a rather strong indication that someone else makes the rules in The City. Dalrymple even depicts a true dream of Sinclair's in contrast with the actuality of The City. It is possible that Sinclair is having a dream within a dream, but it seems more likely that this scene is included to distinguish between Sinclair's real world and his dream world.

The City definitely exists as an independent world. It contains all of the realistic trappings of a metropolis: apartment buildings, high-rises, restaurants and bars, grocery stores and delis, garbage dumps, billboards, and graffiti. But these realistic accoutrements do not make the story any less incredible—remember, after all, how important houses, walls, and yellow brick roads are in *The Wizard of Oz*. Dalrymple is also careful to include some explicitly fantastic elements in his world: The City has Mermaid Rocks, Castle Pond, Angel Cliffs, and the Underworld Hotel. Still, it is its largely realistic setting that allows *Pop Gun War* to complement other literary works rather than just rework them.

Mixed Characters

The characters in the novel are also a mixture of realistic and fantastic, making for fascinating comparisons between texts. In addition to Sinclair, his sister Emily and Addison are realistic characters, as are Koole, the menacing man who steals toys from children, and Rachel, Emily's friend who keeps an eye on Sinclair. The clearly fantastic characters are Sunshine, Percy the pet fish who wears glasses, Mr. Grimshaw, R. K., and the angel. Few of these characters have immediate counterparts in *Peter Pan*, the Alice novels, or the Oz stories, but they do serve the same functions as certain characters in those earlier works, if in a more modern manner. Dalrymple is clearly drawing on these classic novels for inspiration. Addison and Sunshine attempt to guide and mentor Sinclair in the same way that the Scarecrow, the Tin Man, and the Cowardly Lion aid Dorothy. Like those characters, Addison and Sunshine are unusual in some way—they are not "normal" members of society, and the help they provide is not always effective. The wingless angel, who appears mainly at the beginning and end of the novel and who serves as a *deus ex machina*, surely has a parallel in Glinda the Good Witch. Rachel, the most ordinary character in all of *Pop Gun War*, represents a connection to the realistic world, just as Wendy does in *Peter Pan*. Older than Sinclair, she serves as a surrogate mother to him; at the end of Barrie's novel, a grown-up Wendy does the same for Peter. As an animal with human qualities, Percy the fish has many predecessors, most notably the White Rabbit, who also wears glasses, but he may also be compared to *Peter Pan*'s crocodile, who swallows a ticking clock, another aquatic creature permanently stuck with a human-made device. Percy can't talk but is somehow able to communicate with humans; this makes him the opposite of Carroll's dormouse, who can talk but has a hard time communicating sensibly. The thief Koole could reasonably be compared to Captain Hook, pirating the belongings of others and choosing children as his victims. Grimshaw, of course, is borrowed directly from *The Wizard of Oz*. Even minor characters are reminiscent of the earlier novels—Ben Able, the blind private detective, is as self-contradictory in concept as a cowardly lion.

Teachers might ask students to create and employ a "character comparison chart" to track similar characters across texts. Or the teacher might begin such a chart, modeling some examples, and then help students to complete it. Although the examples mentioned in this essay are clearly apparent when the works are read together, students may see additional comparisons between different characters, leading to excellent material for class discussion.

Childhood, Maturity, and Coming of Age—Maybe

Perhaps more important than the characters, however, are the themes that Dalrymple shares with the other works. For example, the conflict between childhood and maturity is important to all of the works. Sinclair's assertion "I'm never getting old" (Dalrymple, 2003, p. 32) is an obvious allusion to *Peter Pan*, but since The City is a more realistic world than Neverland, Sinclair's desire to stay young is different from Peter's. Sinclair has a much greater realization of what he is missing by being young. He can't get into a bar to see his sister sing, and, when Emily disappears for a few days, he has to rely on adults to find her. He is bullied by grown-ups like Mr. Koole and is sometimes frightened for no discernible reason. There is also one odd scene in *Pop Gun War* suggesting that Sinclair has had another existence: Looking into a mirror, he thinks, "Who am I? Who are you? Weird. Have I lived my whole life as this person?" (This self-questioning is perhaps reminiscent of Alice's conversation with the caterpillar.) Then, coming out of his reverie, Sinclair realizes, "Whoa. I almost went crazy there" (Dalrymple, p. 72). It is as if he is experiencing a past life. In other words, Sinclair might not be a child who refuses to grow up; he might be a grown-up who is now in the body of a child.

Emily also suffers as a result of being young. When Grimshaw poses as a journalist and interviews her, one of his questions obviously strikes a nerve: "So what is it like being a child genius? I mean being so young, you . . ." Emily is angered and interrupts him, "Look, can't we talk about something other than my age?" But soon Grimshaw returns to the topic, suggesting that her youth makes her less credible as a musician, "So your critics say you are too young, that you are hiding your immaturity behind cryptic lyrics. Some people resent you for your age." He may just be baiting her, but Emily clearly is disturbed by his remarks; she gets up and leaves the interview altogether (Dalrymple, 2003, p. 60).

Peter Pan enjoys being a child because, in Neverland, he is "captain" and therefore in control. But Sinclair is astute enough to realize that he will never be in control until he is an adult. The reason he doesn't want to get old is that he doesn't want to be like the adults he knows. The ending of *Alice in Wonderland* makes it clear that it is still possible to be happy, even if you're not Peter Pan: you can grow up without losing your essential sense of wonder:

> Lastly she (Alice's sister) pictured to herself how this same little sister of hers would, in the after-time, be herself a grown woman; and how she would keep, through all her riper years, the simple and loving heart of her childhood; and how she would gather about her other little children, and make *their* eyes bright and eager with many a strange tale, perhaps even with the dream of Wonderland of long ago; and how she would feel with all their simple sorrows, and find a pleasure in all their simple joys, remembering her own child-life, and the happy summer days. (Carroll, 1960, p. 116)

It's difficult to believe that Sinclair shares that sentiment; life in The City does not lead to fond memories of childhood. It just creates a fear of growing up to become corrupt or homeless.

Sinclair not only wants to avoid living in the world as an adult, but he also doesn't want to deal with a world that is regimented. Like many children, Sinclair sees rules not as essential elements of a functional society, but only as restrictions on his own freedom—and little boys who fly aren't following the rules. He is wary of the pressures to conform: Emily's refusal to commercialize her music and Addison's dream about doing exactly that with his artwork prove that compromise can be bad. The angel tells Sinclair as much explicitly, stating that he got rid of his wings because "being normal sometimes requires giving up a gift" (Dalrymple, 2003, p. 131). Sinclair doesn't want to give up anything, and he sees no need for compromise since he has never seen anyone benefit from it. Alice, Dorothy, and the Darlings are all happy to return to normal life, whereas Sinclair is disdainful of it.

He also distrusts labels, an element of regimentation. Shortly after he acquires the wings, he accidentally lands in the home of an eccentric man who has labeled everything in the house. Rather than be perturbed that a stranger has flown into his living room, the man eagerly slaps a sign on Sinclair that reads, "boy with wings." "Everything gets a label," the man explains, "because people don't always know what things are" (Dalrymple, 2003, p. 30). But Sinclair, like many real-life teens and adolescents, rejects his label. He flies away, upset and frightened; it is, in fact, this experience that causes him to insist that he will never grow old. Dalrymple provides here an interesting contrast to Alice, who would surely appreciate the labels or, at least, having every word retain a consistent meaning during her adventures. Alice, one of those people who doesn't always know what things are, angers Humpty Dumpty when she calls his cravat a belt. Dumpty, however, isn't so strict with his own word usage, explaining that, "When I use a word, it means just what I choose it to mean, neither more nor less" (Carroll, 1960, p. 186). Alice has a pretty difficult time with semantics at the Mad Tea-Party as well. In *Peter Pan*, there's also a bit of confusion regarding definitions when Wendy briefly convinces Peter that a kiss is a thimble. But again, these characters are living in a more fanciful world; labels have a much greater ability to do harm to Sinclair than they would to these other children. Since modern young people in the outside world must resist labels from the media, their parents, and their peers, it is only logical that students in a class should devote energy to these very literal interpretations of similar pressures in their lives.

In these texts, hand in hand with the conflict between childhood and maturity is the absence of the parent. Dorothy is famously an orphan, reared by her aunt and uncle. Alice's parents are nowhere to be seen in either tale; she is supervised by her older sister. But even Alice's parents are models of responsibility compared to the Darlings, who not only leave their dog Nana in charge of their children—they actually use her as a nurse. "They had a nurse. As they were poor, owing to the amount of milk the children drank, the nurse was a prim Newfoundland dog" (Barrie, 1987, p. 4). This is Barrie being satiric again, of course, but there is no denying that the absence of the parents is an important theme in *Peter Pan*. Peter actively recruits Wendy to Neverland because the lost boys have never known a female and, therefore, have no mother. Peter himself feels rejected when he returns home after an absence of many years and finds his mother attending to her new child. The Darlings go back to England after Wendy realizes that John and Michael have virtually forgotten their parents and have begun to believe that she really is their mother.

Sinclair also has missing parents. His mother is never shown in *Pop Gun War* and is only mentioned once, in a letter Sinclair writes to Emily in which he says, "Mom and I miss you." Otherwise, he might as well be an orphan—maybe he is one and is only referring to his mother in a spiritual sense—there really is no other explanation for her absence other than death, particularly when Emily goes missing for days and Sinclair asks everyone he knows where she might be, never turning to his mother. Deceased parents would also explain a dream Sinclair describes to Rachel, in which he attends his parents' wedding and dances with his mother: "It didn't matter that I hadn't been born yet. The memory was real. And very dear to me" (Dalrymple, 2003, p. 19). It seems safe to say that any child who has a dream like that has serious psychological issues stemming from the absence of the parents—and, once again, the fact that Sinclair lives in a somewhat realistic world makes his lack of parental guidance different from that of Alice, Dorothy, or Peter. Sinclair can't avoid real world problems, so his lack of parents doesn't allow him to stay young, despite his vow. To the contrary, it causes him to grow up more quickly so that he can deal with these problems. This is underscored at the novel's end, when Addison, an adult, has to ask Sinclair for advice. This is also why Sinclair sees himself in an adult role at his parents' wedding.

Bonus Teaching Idea

In the fall of 2000, James Bucky Carter taught Alice in Wonderland *to a group of high school seniors in western North Carolina who were taking a course called Honors English Literature. He noted that most of the students were simultaneously enrolled in an introductory psychology course where they were learning about human development. "Using that to my advantage, I introduced the text as an example of a person waffling between being a frivolous and silly child and a more mature, thoughtful young woman. I shared an overhead of Piaget's stages of cognitive development*

Continued

with the class and asked them to note how Alice handled certain situations as the text developed. Was she growing? Could we see evidence of her move from the concrete operational stage, for example, and into the formal operational stage? We analyzed the text from an educational psychologist's point of view!" (Carter, personal communication, May 30, 2005). This idea could be similarly applied to Peter, the Darlings, Dorothy, and the characters in Pop Gun War.

Escape

Ultimately, all of these novels are about something that children value greatly, namely, escape—from rules, from school (although it is rarely mentioned in any of these works), from parents, from growing up. Dorothy leaves Kansas for a world in which she has more power and control than she ever had back home. Many literary scholars have interpreted Alice's adventures as being the symbolic depiction of a girl's entrance into puberty, using her visits to other worlds to deal with very real physical and emotional issues. After leaving Neverland, Wendy returns there twice; her daughter and granddaughter also visit regularly, easing the transition into adulthood. And Sinclair flies high above The City, putting aside for a while the problems that trouble him, his sister, and everyone else he knows. As with the use of labels, this shared element of the texts calls out for analysis and discussion because young readers and teachers alike can relate to the idea of wanting or needing to escape every once in a while.

Conclusions

Good fantasies have morals. The morals to the three already-classic novels are essentially the same: no matter how fanciful the fantasy world might be, home is better, and, at some point, the child will gladly return there. *Pop Gun War* has a different moral. It has to be a different moral because, although Alice, the Darlings, and Dorothy do have the option of leaving at some point—Sinclair does not. He never left the real world to visit a fantasy; his real world and his fantasy coexist. His story is not about returning home, but about surviving home. *Pop Gun War*'s moral can be found in Sinclair's final line: "These wings have always been mine" (Dalrymple, 2003, p. 134). Rather than exploring another world, he has explored the self and discovered something valuable. And Sinclair's tale is ultimately different because it is a graphic representation. By exploring *Pop Gun War* in relation to the three printed texts, teachers and students can explore uncanny worlds while investigating common themes and shared experiences of characters. The unique format of the graphic novel creates the opportunity for observing how fictions are crafted and how texts with similar themes can approach those themes from different formal traditions.

References

Barrie, J. M. (1987). *Peter Pan*. New York: Signet.

Carroll, L. (1960). *Alice's adventures in Wonderland & Through the looking glass*. New York: Signet.

Dalrymple, F. (2003) *Pop Gun War*. Milwaukie, OR: Dark Horse Comics.

7 Abandon Every Fear, Ye That Enter: The X-Men Journey through Dante's *Inferno*

Don Leibold
Loyola Academy, Milwaukee, Wisconsin,
a Milwaukee Public Schools Partnership High School

Introduction: Into the Pit!

Fierce winds rage against a rocky, foreboding landscape. The Uncanny X-Men, Marvel Comics' popular band of mutant heroes, and their comrade, Sorcerer Supreme Doctor Strange, stand before a monstrous door with a lengthy inscription ending with the words, "Abandon every hope, ye that enter." A disorienting transdimensional journey has left the X-Men dazed and shaken; they look to Doctor Strange for guidance. He offers: "This is the gateway to Hell, as described by the 14th-century Italian poet, Dante Alighieri in his classic poem, *The Inferno*. That epic chronicled Dante's descent into the pit, and his eventual meeting with Satan himself. It seems we're expected to follow in his footsteps" (Claremont, Romita, & McLeod, 1980, p. 12). So starts "Nightcrawler's Inferno," a story in which the X-Men journey into what they believe to be Dante's hellish realm.

The Gateway

I first read "Nightcrawler's Inferno" when it was originally published in 1980 in *X-Men Annual #4*. I was nine years old. Nearly twenty-five years later, after rereading *X-Men Annual #4* as reprinted in *Essential X-Men Volume 3*, I was inspired, finally, to read *The Inferno*. After noticing the inventive ways that writer Chris Claremont incorporated elements of Dante's work into his own, I began to see "Nightcrawler's Inferno" as a gateway text for the English classroom. Indeed, other teacher-scholars have noticed a strong pedagogical content in the X-Men series. Shirley Brice Heath and Vikram Bhagat (1997) note the complex vocabulary and often literary themes used in the series: "The *X-Men* comic books, therefore, defy traditional assumptions regarding the nature of comic books and the 'low-level' skills necessary to read them" (p. 588). The specific potential-laden "gateway" of which I speak (see Figure 7.1) would not require that young readers abandon hope; on the contrary, it could give readers hope in the form of background information and points of comparison as they tackle a complex, canonical work. Teachers willing to pair this X-Men story with Dante's classic work might find that their students' appreciation of both texts would develop considerably sooner than it did for me.

Meet the Heroes

Since not everyone is familiar with the X-Men, here are some character sketches. Use them to introduce key team members or to get students predicting the fates of the heroes as the story progresses. After sharing the descriptions, consider asking students to speculate on what "sins" each character might be guilty of and, once students learn of Dante's infernal layers, what circle of the Inferno he or she might have trouble escaping. More information on all of the heroes can be found by visiting http:// www.marvel.com.

***Colossus:** "Peter Rasputin" can turn his body into organic steel that makes him very strong and hard to injure. He is a quiet, artistic man who sometimes feels he should be back home helping on the family farm in Russia rather than in the United States. His guilt and uncertainty match his naivety, but he has a loving heart and loyal spirit.*

***Dr. Strange:** "Stephen" is not usually associated with the X-Men. He is a sorcerer and deals with all of the magic-related elements of the Marvel Universe. He feels pressure to do his job well because he is one of the only heroes responsible for keeping order on multiple planes of existence.*

***Nightcrawler:** "Kurt Wagner" has the ability to teleport and has skin so indigo in color that he can blend in with shadows. He is a devout Catholic and often acts as the team's conscience, but he is frequently conflicted in his role as a hero and as a Christian. He is often insecure about his place in the world but hides it behind a suave, humorous attitude.*

***Pryde, Kitty:** A teenage mutant with the ability to become intangible, Kitty is new to the team in this adventure and wonders if she can handle the pressure of being a full-time member. She has a tenacious spirit, however, and her last name says something about her character.*

Continued

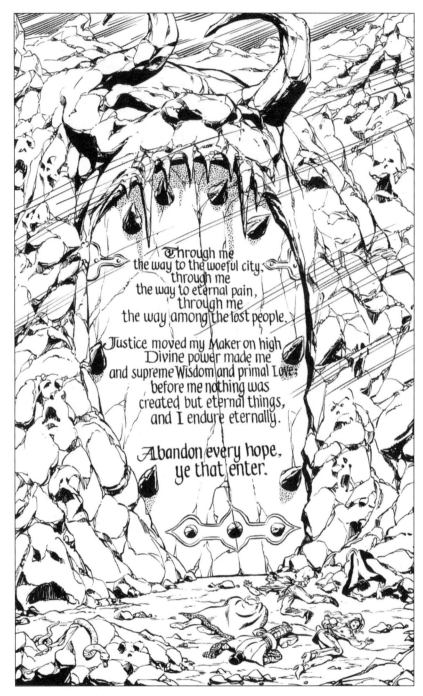

Figure 7.1. A panel from *X-Men Annual #4,* "Nightcrawler's Inferno," that reflects strong connections to Dante's *Inferno.*

> **Storm:** *"Ororo Monroe" once thought she was a goddess and sometimes has trouble remembering she isn't. She has the ability to control the weather, but her temperament is as uncertain as the weather.*
>
> **Wolverine:** *"Logan" is a short, stocky man with a bad attitude and razor sharp claws coming out of the backs of his hands. He often loses control of his temper and sometimes seems uncaring.*
>
> **Xavier, Charles:** *This professor is the X-Men's wheelchair-bound leader. He is often an absent presence in their adventures, but his leadership is what guides them. He has the ability to read minds and believes that mutants and humans can coexist peacefully. Some think he named the X-Men after himself. Since he is a telepath, he often deals with issues of moral integrity in how he should and should not use his powers.*

Background and Review: Dante Alighieri and *The Inferno*

The Inferno is part of a trilogy written by Dante Alighieri, an Italian poet who wrote during the fourteenth century. Each section explores a different environment of the Christian/Catholic afterlife: *The Inferno, Purgatory*, and *Paradise*. Collectively, the works are referred to as *The Divine Comedy*. In *The Inferno*, Dante envisions Hell as a pit, divided into nine concentric circles, each housing a class of sinners. As one descends from circle to circle, the number of sinners grows smaller, the sins grow more heinous, and the punishments more fiendishly appropriate. Sections and subsections of Hell and their attendant penalties are described in vivid, grisly detail in the poem's thirty-four cantos. (See Figure 7.2.)

Dante chose not to write these works in Latin, the preferred literary tongue of the time, but in the Tuscan Italian dialect of his hometown, Florence, to make them accessible to the common person. Dante's decision should resonate with comic book readers, since they read and enjoy texts that, despite growing respectability, are still met with skepticism by some academics, teachers, and other cultural gatekeepers.

Connections with "Nightcrawler's Inferno"

The connections between "Nightcrawler's Inferno" and Dante's *Inferno* are numerous. Not only are both clear examples of allegory, but *X-Men* writer Chris Claremont was clearly paying homage: the X-Men story includes numerous references and allusions to Dante's poem. The Marvel Universe's resident sorcerer, Doctor Strange, acts as the X-Men's

Figure 7.2. A scene from Hell in "Nightcrawler's Inferno."

guide through their journey in Hell, just as Virgil, author of *The Aeneid*, acts as Dante's guide. Prominent *Inferno* characters such as Charon, Minos, Cerberus, the Harpies, and Satan are featured in the X-Men story. Thematic elements are prevalent as well. Two X-Men team members, Colossus, an atheist, and Nightcrawler, a devout Catholic, briefly debate the need for a Hell. Likewise, characters ponder their personal relationship to the "punishment must match the crime" theme apparent in both texts. Wolverine, a hero prone to fits of animalistic rage, silently ruminates on a possible future in the Fifth Circle of Hell, home to souls of the wrathful. Early on, Storm, a former teen pickpocket, is cast down into the pit and found later in the Seventh Bolgia of the Eighth Circle, where thieves are punished.

Doctor Strange and the X-Men pass through the first three levels—Caina, Antenora, Ptolomea—without incident and with the Sorcerer Supreme acting as a perfect teacher to X-Men and students alike. Doctor Strange informs the team that Caina, named for the biblical character Cain, who murdered his brother Abel, is reserved for "those who betrayed their kindred" (Claremont et al., 1980, p. 29). Antenora, named for the Trojan prince who was believed to have schemed with the Greeks to destroy his own city, is intended for "traitors to their country or cause" (p. 29). Ptolomea is named for Ptolomy, the captain of Jericho who invited high priest Simon Maccabee and his sons to his home for dinner only to murder them. This third level is for "hosts who betrayed their guests," Doctor Strange informs the X-Men (p. 29).

When the heroes set foot on the bottom of the pit, a place called Judecca, Nightcrawler is struck by a bolt of black lightning and instantaneously encased in the ice floor of the Inferno. This fourth level, Judecca, is host to "any who broke faith with their lords or benefactors" (Claremont et al., 1980, p. 29). In Dante's *Inferno*, only three souls reside here: Brutas, Cassius, and Judas. Brutas and Cassius conspired to murder Julius Caesar, who, after the defeat of Pompey, pardoned the two men and awarded them with prestigious titles. Judas Iscariot betrayed Jesus Christ to the Roman authorities for thirty pieces of silver, even though he was chosen by Christ to be one of his Twelve Apostles. In "Nightcrawler's Inferno," Nightcrawler is treated as a traitor as well. Here the stories diverge, however, because Nightcrawler is not quite as deserving of this fate as Dante's crew. Soon it is revealed that Nightcrawler's surrogate mother, Margali Szardos, a powerful sorceress whose abilities humble even Doctor Strange, has created an imposter Inferno to punish Nightcrawler for the murder of her first-born son, Stefan, and the betrayal of her love and trust. Kurt Wagner (Nightcrawler's given name) and Stefan had grown close and become blood brothers. Sensing latent evil in his own soul, Stefan had made Kurt vow to kill him if he ever murdered an innocent person. Years later, Stefan commits a series of murders, forcing Kurt to confront him. While engaged in hand-to-hand combat, Stefan's neck snaps and he dies instantly. In this way, Nightcrawler accidentally kept his vow to Stefan, but his surrogate mother doesn't see Stefan's death as accidental. Reminiscent of Dante's Satan, she is happy to see the sinner devoured by his sins.

The End of Exile

Although Dante's real-life exile never ended, the fictional Dante does find a way out of Hell, after observing Lucifer torturing the three souls in Judecca. He and his guide, Virgil, follow the hole that was created by Lucifer when he fell to, and into, the Earth. They emerge on the other side of the planet and see the stars in the night sky. Nightcrawler's banishment to his own personal Inferno and his accompanying estrangement from the maternal Margali Szardos ends as well. After learning the true nature of the death of her son, Szardos forgives Nightcrawler. He and his fellow adventurers are magically returned to their home in Xavier's mansion.

Home

Countless fans find second homes at their local comic book shops. In his book, *Comic Book Culture: Fanboys and True Believers*, Matthew J. Pustz (1999) examines the comic book fan community. He concludes that comic book fans are participants in a small, but thriving cultural community that celebrates literacy, storytelling, visual expression, and text-based debate. This resonates directly with Standard 11 of *Standards for the English Language Arts* (2005) as established by NCTE and the International Reading Association: "Students participate as knowledgeable, reflective, creative, and critical members of a variety of literacy communities." The X-Men titles, one of the most popular and successful comic book franchises ever, may be the catalyst for the creation of a group of student fans: pairing "Nightcrawler's Inferno" with Dante's timeless work is a powerful way to promote the growth of a literacy community in the classroom.

The following sections provide more information on the texts and suggestions for how teachers might explore them. First, a discussion of allegory in each tale is considered; then a series of activities is suggested. Finally, I offer an extensive list of endnotes detailing references to *The Inferno* in the X-Men story.

Allegory and the X-Men

Since issue #1 of *The X-Men* was published in 1963, the comic and its countless satellite titles function together as an allegory for racism and cultural intolerance (Wein, 2006). Most of Marvel's mutants, like various citizen groups demanding their civil rights in the United States in the 1960s, struggle to convince the mainstream human population that they should be accorded a place in that society. Some mutants, notably X-Men archenemy Magneto, see such a struggle as futile. They prefer instead to take militant action to secure two goals: self-preservation and the creation of a mutant-centric society. These themes are highlighted in the *X-Men* movie released in 2000. Professor Xavier advocates for assimilation in the way of Martin Luther King, Jr., whereas Magneto, taking his cues from Malcolm X, embodies a radical, aggressive agenda. At one point, Magneto even utters the Malcolm X credo, "By any means necessary."

Allegory and *The Inferno*

An allegory has two parallel functions: to tell a story and to illuminate issues and concerns of the culture that birthed the story and its writer. The *X-Men* comics collectively function as a humanist allegory for life in a multicultural society that is struggling with issues of tolerance and justice. Dante's journey through Hell in *The Inferno* functions as an allegory as well. He begins the poem with these words:

> Midway upon the journey of our life
> I found myself within a forest dark,
> For the straightforward pathway had been lost (Canto I, 1–3)

"Life is a journey" is a common but powerful metaphor that humans use to organize their experiences. Joseph Campbell (1968) explored this metaphor in his book *The Hero with a Thousand Faces*. After analyzing various mythologies from cultures around the globe, he titled the dominant, shared storyline, "The Hero's Journey." By evoking this archetypal narrative and by making himself the hero, Dante makes it clear to the reader that his work is an allegory. Later in Canto IX, Dante even offers his own poetic definition of allegory:

> O ye who have distempered intellects,
> Observe the doctrine that conceals itself
> Beneath the veil of the mysterious verses! (Canto IX, 61–63)

The English translation used here is by Henry Wadsworth Longfellow, as published by Barnes & Noble Classics. John Ciardi's translation, published as part of the Modern Library Series, actually uses the word "allegory" where Longfellow uses "verses." (Note that there is also a recent translation [2005] by Georges Pruteanu available on the Internet.)

The "doctrine" Dante mentions in Canto IX is the Christian theology, specifically Catholicism. Just as the X-Men are a product of the 1960s in the United States, Dante is a product of his own time and place. The turn of the fourteenth century in Florence was a similarly tumultuous time. Florence, the capital of Tuscany and the birthplace of the Italian Renaissance, was grappling with the role of the Pope in the community. Dante was elected Prior, the city's highest office, in 1300. By 1302, respect for him had declined. His party, the Guelphs, had split over issues of church and state. One faction, the Whites, opposed any involvement in Florentine politics on the part of Pope Boniface VIII and his representative, Charles of Valois. The Blacks, conversely, welcomed papal participation. Dante, a White, was exiled when the Blacks took control of the government in 1302. Although he never returned to Florence, he did not forget the city. Several allusions to Florentine politics are made in *The Inferno*. In Canto XXVI, Dante seemingly praises Florence for earning renown on Earth and in Hell, although the hyperbole he employs cues the reader to interpret his words as sarcasm:

> Rejoice, O Florence, since thou art so great,
> That over sea and land thou beatest thy wings,
> And throughout Hell thy name is spread abroad! (Canto XXVI, 1–3)

By incorporating Florentine political references into *The Inferno*, Dante solidifies the work's allegorical nature. Although a devout Catholic, Dante, and his fellow Whites, believed that a line should be drawn between the government and the church. He exorcises his resentment over the treachery he was subjected to at the hands of the Blacks by depicting their comeuppance in Hell. His imaginative creation comments directly on the real world.

In a more general way, *The Inferno* reflects Dante's Catholic faith. Dante wanted his readers to think about their behaviors and attitudes—this likely explains why he eschewed Latin for his native Tuscan dialect. He enthusiastically detailed the wages of sin, a key component of Christian theology, as a way to influence society.

If Dante and Nightcrawler Could Discuss Allegory

Dante would likely agree with Nightcrawler when he says, "Hell is balanced by Heaven. And those who come here deserve their damnation" (Claremont et al. 1980, p. 25). For each sin named in *The Inferno*, Dante crafts a brutally clever penalty. In the Forest of the Suicides in the Seventh Circle, souls who rejected their bodies via self-murder are trapped in trees. From these trees dangle the spurned bodies for the souls to ponder for eternity. Fortune-tellers are trapped in the Eighth Circle. Because in life they sought to see the future, these souls must walk with their heads on backward and tears in their eyes. In pairing *The Inferno* with *X-Men*, the teacher might want to point out an important difference: the X-Men do not deserve the hellish treatment they receive in their own allegorical existence.

Classroom Activities

The following activities are designed with a few general precepts in mind: learning occurs when students discuss and debate, when they create something or take some action, and when teachers give them a reasonable amount of freedom. For the greatest degree of intellectual freedom, teachers might want to avoid specifying a genre of writing for a given project. For example, Activity 2 asks students to consider this question: Are all of the sinners Dante mentions in *The Inferno* deserving of a place in Hell? A student could respond to this question with an essay, a speech, a poem, a skit, or a comic strip. Any of these products could be created by a student alone or in concert with a partner or small group. Teachers and students thrive in an environment where they make choices that suit their needs and desires. (The University of Texas at Austin's *Danteworlds* website, http://danteworlds.laits.utexas.edu/, is a handy resource for post-reading activities.)

1. Map of Hell
Provide students with two sets of cards: one labeled with words naming the types of sins/sinners that are mentioned in *The Inferno*, the other with definitions for the words in the first card set. Students should pair each word with its definition. After familiarizing themselves with these key words, have them rank the sins/sinners from least heinous to most heinous. It is important that the students record their rankings, because

after reading *The Inferno* they will be asked to reassess their rankings using a blank "Map of Hell" modeled after Gustav Doré's own "Map of Hell," found on the page directly following the Introduction in Barnes & Noble Classic's 2003 edition of *The Inferno*. Or students can find their own model "Map of Hell" on the Internet by doing an image search with a search engine.

2. Crime and Punishment
Are all of the sinners Dante mentions in *The Inferno* deserving of a place in Hell? Ask students to defend Dante by picking a type of sinner mentioned in the poem and explaining why such a person deserves to be punished for eternity. Or have students critique Dante and make a case for excluding certain types of sinners from an eternity in Hell.

3. The Hero's Journey
Ask students to look for the elements of Joseph Campbell's "Hero's Journey" in Dante's journey through the Inferno. How does *The Inferno* conform to Campbell's outline? How does it diverge from it?

4. More with Allegory
The X-Men comic books function as an allegory for life in a multicultural society facing questions of tolerance and justice. *The Inferno* is a Christian allegory that, at times, comments on fourteenth-century Italian politics. Ask students to name another example of such an allegory and to provide proof for how the text conforms to the definition of "allegory."

5. Comic/Canon Connection
Does another issue/story from *Essential X-Men Volume 3* resonate with another work of literature? Ask students to detail the connections between the two texts. Ask students how well they think the comic book form portrays the Inferno. If Dante had used the comic book format to tell his story, how would it have been different? Do students appreciate seeing Claremont and Cockrum's version of Dante's Hell? Or do they prefer it when they read the printed version alone and can therefore visualize how things look on their own? Does the comic book version allow for anything unique that other forms of adaptation might not be able to capture?

6. Supervillains and Dante
Ask students to consider the X-Men villains featured in *Essential X-Men Volume 3*. Of what sins would Dante find them guilty? To what places in Hell would they be assigned? The major villains in the book are, in order of appearance, Doctor Doom, Arcade, Magneto, Sebastian Shaw/

the Black King, Emma Frost/the White Queen, Deathbird, Rogue, Dracula, Belasco, and Baron Strucker. Students may find a visit to http://www.marvel.com a compelling way to learn more about these villains, thereby helping them craft well-informed answers. Wikipedia (http://www.wikipedia.com) is also an impressive resource for information on comic characters.

7. *Dante Goes to Hollywood*
Wizard, a magazine publication that covers the comic book industry, often runs a feature in which the editors play casting director and choose actors for parts in upcoming comic book movie adaptations or ones they would like to see. Ask students to cast a movie adaptation of Dante's *Inferno*. Who should play Dante? Virgil? Charon? Each casting choice must be accompanied by a rationale.

8. *Dante Meets Nightcrawler*
Ask students to write a brief skit in which Nightcrawler and Dante compare notes on their experiences in their respective Infernos. The two can discuss similarities and differences. Students can consider adding Margali Szardos to the skit as well. Dante might enjoy arguing with her about alterations she made to his Inferno. For example, Brutas, Cassius, and Judas are missing from the Ninth Circle.

9. *The Backpack*
Both Dante and Nightcrawler begin their journeys with little preparation. Ask students to imagine a trip to the Inferno with a backpack full of supplies. What would be in the backpack? Provide a rationale for each item packed.

10. *Rating Systems*
The Inferno is not for the faint-hearted reader. It contains graphic violence, nudity, and scatological references. Many editions feature illustrations that clearly depict these phenomena. Ask students to research the rating systems for movies, television shows, and video games. Then have them develop a rating system for books. Finally, using that rating system, students can assign a rating to *The Inferno* and construct a defense of that rating.

11. The Inferno *as Comic Strip*
Transform one of *The Inferno*'s thirty-four cantos into a comic strip. Ask students to prepare for the task by researching the conventions of comic books and sequential art. Scott McCloud's *Understanding Comics: The Invisible Art* and Will Eisner's *Comics and Sequential Art* are ideal places to start.

References

Alighieri, D. (1996). *The Inferno*. Trans. John Ciardi. New York: Modern Library.

Alighieri, D. (2002). *The Inferno*. Trans. Anthony Esolen. New York: Modern Library.

Alighieri, D. (2003). *The Inferno*. Trans. Henry Wadsworth Longfellow. New York: Barnes & Noble Classics.

Alighieri, D. (2005). Canto V. *The Inferno*. Trans. George Pruteanu. Retrieved July 14, 2005, from http://www.pruteanu.ro/Dante/cint05-4lb.htm

Campbell, J. (1968). *The Hero with a Thousand Faces* (2nd ed.). Princeton, NJ: Princeton University Press.

Claremont, C., & Cockrum, D. (2001). *The Essential X-Men vol. III: Uncanny X-Men #145–161 and X-Men Annuals #3–5.* New York: Marvel Comics.

Claremont, C., Romita, J., Jr., & McLeod, B. (1980). Nightcrawler's inferno. *The Uncanny X-Men Annual #4.* New York: Marvel Comics.

Danteworlds. (2004.) Guy P. Raffa (Ed.). University of Texas at Austin. Retrieved July 14, 2005, from http://danteworlds.laits.utexas.edu/

Heath, S. B., & Bhagat. V. (1997). Reading comics, the invisible art. In *Handbook of research on teaching literacy through the communicative and visual arts* (Vol. 1, pp. 586–59). New York: Macmillan Library Reference USA.

Pustz, M. J. (1999). Comic book culture: Fanboys and true believers. Jackson, MS: University of Mississippi Press.

NCTE. (2005). Standards for the English language arts. Retrieved July 14, 2005, from http://www.ncte.org/about/over/standards/110846.htm

Singer, B. (Director). (2000). *X-Men* [Motion picture]. Beverly Hills, CA: Twentieth-Century Fox.

Virgil. (1990). *The Aeneid*. Trans. Robert Fitzgerald. New York: Vintage.

Wein, L. (2006). (Ed.). *The unauthorized X-Men: SF and comic writers on mutants, prejudice, and adamantium*. Dallas: Benbella Books.

8 A Multimodal Approach to Addressing Antisemitism: Charles Dickens's *Oliver Twist* and Will Eisner's *Fagin the Jew*

Allen Webb and Brandon Guisgand
Western Michigan University

The mud lay thick upon the stones, and a black mist hung over the streets; the rain fell sluggishly down, and everything felt cold and clammy to the touch. It seemed just the night when it befitted such a being as the Jew to be abroad. As he glided stealthily along, creeping beneath the shelter of the walls and doorways, the hideous old man seemed like some loathsome reptile, engendered in the slime and darkness through which he moved, crawling forth by night in search of some rich offal for a meal.

Oliver Twist

Charles Dickens's ever-popular *Oliver Twist*, first published as a best-selling magazine serial from 1837 to 1839, continues to have a remarkable career in the multimedia age. There have been more than twenty movie and television versions, including a new 2005 film directed by Roman Polanski; the Broadway musical "Oliver;" retellings such as "Oliver Junior;" cartoon versions from Looney Tunes to the Muppets; and a host of online digitized texts, all searchable, some hypertexted or otherwise interactive. Yet, despite its popularity, as we will elaborate, the story of *Oliver Twist* is deeply troubling. Drawing on antisemitic[1] themes and functioning as part of a long and ugly tradition of antisemitic writing, *Oliver Twist* was condemned in its own day. Given the continued interest in the novel, we wonder whether part of the draw of the story, in its day and in the present, might not in fact be its antisemitism, its problematic treatment of the attractive/repulsive anti-hero, Fagin, and his frightening relationship with the destitute orphan boys. Investigating the appeal and implications of the novel, we contend that the contradictions and questions raised by it are the key to making the teaching of *Oliver Twist* meaningful to high school and college readers in the twenty-first century.

In 2003, one of the founders of the graphic novel genre, Will Eisner, created a graphic novel version of *Oliver Twist* called *Fagin the Jew,* which precisely focuses on the issue of the representation of Fagin and the question of antisemitism in Dickens's day. The graphic novel format, which develops the narrative extensively by illustration, raises and explores questions of cultural representation in ways that make multimodal comparisons with Dickens's classic novel and other antisemitic images and texts especially compelling. Taking the graphic novel form seriously means examining it not in isolation as a unique or peculiar genre, but considering it in the broader context of the literary, historical, and cultural documents, both textual and visual, of which it is a part and to which it offers a complex and important response. This kind of analysis draws on the appeal of the graphic novel in the classroom and engages students in meaningful cultural studies in which traditional literary study is only a part.

Oliver Twist sets forward the story of a boy of upper-class parentage who is cast down into poverty. Challenging the hypocritical moralism of the Poor Laws, Dickens's sympathetic hero asks the question, "Please Sir, can I have a little more?" Escaping the brutality of the nineteenth-century English workhouse, a penniless Oliver makes his way to London, where he becomes the victim of a ring of pickpockets. The group is masterminded by Fagin, "the Jew," who dominates the boys with a mixture of charm, trickery, and threatened violence in order to build his hoard of stolen watches, jewelry, and gold. Held captive in Fagin's fallen world of crime and moral degradation—the dark underside of the emerging industrial metropolis—Oliver is finally rescued by the goodly Mr. Brownlow and restored, through Christian charity, to happiness and his proper social position. Fagin, on the other hand, is condemned to death by hanging—an event welcomed by the citizens of London: "The building rang with a tremendous shout, and another, and another, and then it echoed loud groans, then gathered strength as they swelled out, like angry thunder. It was a peal of joy from the populace outside, greeting the news that he would die on Monday" (p. 469).

A long history of antisemitism in both image and text precedes *Oliver Twist* and provides the fundamental plot, characterizations, and settings on which the novel is based. During the Middle Ages, antisemitic attitudes were rationalized by biblical verses depicting Jewish peoples as immoral and as "killers of Christ." The Crusades were a bitter and prolonged ordeal for the Jews of Europe as well as for the

Muslim rivals of the Roman Church. It was in this context that the massacre at York, for instance, occurred in 1190:

> The ignorant mobs were incited by the leaders of the Crusades to pillage and massacre whole Jewish communities. The cry was: "Before attempting to revenge ourselves upon the Moslem unbelievers, let us first revenge ourselves upon the 'killers of Christ' living in our midst!" Thousands of Jews perished, and entire Jewish communities were wiped out. To this day, the Jewish liturgy contains prayers commemorating the martyrs of that dreadful period. (Bridger, 1976, p. 101)

Wealthy Christians, forbidden by the Church from lending money, supported Jewish money lenders, tax and debt collectors, and traders in gems and precious commodities. Forced to live in separated communities (the word "ghetto" comes from the name given to the Jewish neighborhood in Venice), Jews were seen as ugly, unscrupulous, and detestable and were considered religious, ethnic, and racial "others." Antisemitic literature, sermons, and stories were widely circulated, which fed stereotypes, persecution, expulsions, and pogroms. In times of economic hardship, Jews were made scapegoats, blamed and castigated for conditions or events that they likely had nothing to do with.

   Antisemitic stories from this period make for disturbing comparisons with *Oliver Twist*. One such example is Chaucer's "Prioress' Tale," one of the *Canterbury Tales* written near the year 1400. In the story, a Jewish community "Hateful to Crist" is established in a medieval town. A young boy, son of a widow, attends a school near the community and passes alone through the Jewish neighborhood singing Christian songs. Offended by the songs, Jews capture the boy in an alley, cut his throat, and throw him into a cesspool (see Figure 8.1). His widowed mother seeks her son, yet none of the Jews will reveal what happened. According to Chaucer's story, Christ puts into her mind an idea of where to look for her son, and she discovers his body. A miracle takes place, and, although the boy is dead and his throat cut, he begins once more to sing Christian songs—and continues singing until he is taken up to heaven. The town leader declares that all of the Jews who knew of the boy's murder be torn apart by horses and then hanged. The tale ends with a reference to the "cursed Jewes" who also killed the child Hugh of Lincoln (another similar tale).

   Notice the many commonalities with *Oliver Twist*. A young, innocent, faithful Christian boy missing his parents enters the wrong part of town, where deceptive, filthy Jews capture and abuse or kill him. By Christian charity and near miraculous discovery, the boy is saved, the

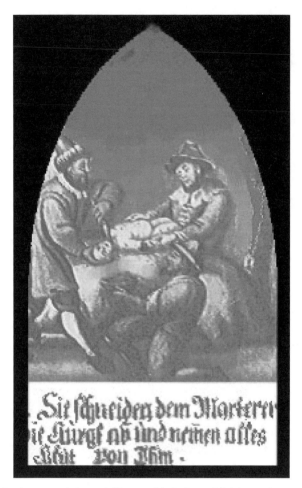

Figure 8.1. An image of Jews killing a Christian child (1462).

Jews are killed, and moral order is restored. It is the kind of story that, repeated over and over in different forms and contexts, generates powerful conscious attitudes and unconscious feelings in some people and can serve to generate and justify antisemitic discrimination and violence. For instance, wide circulation of stories of this kind led to the expulsion of Jews from England in 1290.

     Antisemitism is an important topic for the language arts or social studies classroom in the high school. Understanding the mentality, attitude, and philosophy that develop antisemitic ideology and help bring about racism and violence is equally or more important for students to learn about than the Nazi Holocaust itself. Different forms of racism have different origins, but the study of antisemitism, one of the oldest and most persistent forms of discrimination, provides an in-depth understanding of intolerance and racism in general. In addition to the *Canterbury Tales,* other classic literary works raise questions of antisemitism. There is, of course, the far richer but still stereotypical portrait of a Jew in Shakespeare's *Merchant of Venice,* and problematic portrayals can be found in George Eliot's *Daniel Deronda* and in the poetry of Ezra Pound and T. S. Eliot. The investigation of antisemitism calls for examining literary works in a broader cultural studies context, one for which there are a wide variety of materials that can be used in the classroom. Many texts and images in the disturbing history of antisemitism can be found on the Internet, as well as in libraries and Jewish resource centers. The writing of Charles Dickens, so commonly included in the secondary school curriculum, is, unfortunately, a relevant place to begin this examination. Graphic novels—including *Maus* by Art Spiegelman and *Fagin the Jew* by Will Eisner—are important resources for the investigation.

Antisemitism in *Oliver Twist* is not merely a contemporary problem of "political correctness." In July 1863, Dickens received a letter from Eliza Davis, a woman to whom he had sold his home, raising the question of "the great wrong" Dickens had done to the "Jewish people" in his depiction of Fagin in *Oliver Twist*, encouraging "a vile prejudice against the despised Hebrew." He responded by claiming that Fagin was a historically accurate "representative of a race not a religion," a Jew "because he is one of the Jewish people, and because it conveys that kind of idea of him which I should give my readers of a Chinaman by calling him Chinese." Dickens defended his novel: "It unfortunately was true of the time to which the story refers that that class of criminal almost invariably was a Jew."[2] Even in Dickens's effort to defend the portrayal of Fagin (see Figure 8.2), we can see the influence of racism and an antisemitic interpretation of history. If these ideas had their forbearers in antisemitism before Dickens, they were only exacerbated by nineteenth-century racist "science"—biology and eugenics such as Arthur de Gobineau's essay *The Inequality of the Human Races* (1853–1855), published sixteen years after *Oliver Twist* and before Dickens's exchange of letters with Eliza Davis, which argues for the superiority of the "Aryan race."

Dickens himself may have had some sense of the inadequacy of his justification for writing *Oliver Twist*. Two years after the Eliza Davis letters, Dickens published *Our Mutual Friend* (1865), a work in which the polarity of the Jewish stereotype is reversed. In this novel, a Chris-

Figure 8.2. Fagin, by George Cruickshank, from the first edition of *Oliver Twist.*

tian is the moneylender and slum landlord, and a Jew is his unwilling front man. If having a Christian serve as the cause of stereotypical Jewish behavior is less offensive, it still falls short, failing to explore the complexities of stereotype. Perhaps still unsatisfied, Dickens later reworked *Oliver Twist* for a new edition thirty years after the original publication. In this version, Dickens eliminates the bulk of repeated references to "the Jew" and replaces them with "he" or "Fagin"—removing "the Jew" from fifty-three references in two chapters alone. (Current editions of *Oliver Twist* typically follow the original version, with "the Jew" references intact.) A question that students might explore is how a change in references to Fagin influences, if at all, the overall antisemitic issues in the novel.

One of the major problems of antisemitism in *Oliver Twist* is the way that Fagin serves as a scapegoat, taking the blame for the very real and disturbing issues of poverty and wealth that Dickens brings to the fore. Although Dickens effectively criticizes the hypocrisy of the poor-house and its failure to meet even minimal standards of decency in the first chapters, the sentimental ending of the novel provides only a romantic solution for Oliver and makes no suggestion about how to better the lives of the many other poor boys in the novel—other than the hanging of Fagin. When Allen Webb taught *Oliver Twist* in an introductory university literature course on homelessness,[3] the students were not only able to think critically about the stereotyping of Fagin, they also began to see how Jewish stereotypes were connected to poverty and homelessness in England. Through discussion, they considered how the stereotypical treatment of Fagin not only misrepresents Jews but casts the evil of the social situation onto a particular, flawed individual. The idea of a conspiracy of Jews stealing from the middle classes, hoarding wealth, and threatening the social and economic order recalls to the modern reader the "pawnbroker" scapegoating and global banking conspiracy theories that Hitler used and to which contemporary neo-Nazis continue to refer.

Great Expectations, one of the most commonly taught novels in high schools in the United States, is also flawed by an antisemitic stereotype. The character Habraham Latharuth is a fawning, money hungry, untrustworthy Jew with a lisp and a repulsive demeanor. Teachers who use the version of the novel as it is serialized in textbooks may not be familiar with Habraham Latharurth because the character has been expurgated from the school textbook versions. Although this censorship may be understandable, providing students with a complete text, as Dickens wrote it, and then helping them examine the text critically seems like a more responsible and productive approach. Teachers who are using the censored textbook version and who want to address antisemitism can, of course, bring portions from the original version into the class. When Allen Webb taught the complete text of *Great Expectations* to ninth graders, they found a close reading of the antisemitic scenes to be enlightening. Learning about the Jewish stereotyping in the novel led one student to ask, weeks later, if the obviously humorous "Aged Parent" at the end of the novel might not also be a stereotyped depiction of older people. The "Jewish question," as it is referred to, can also be examined in Dickens's *The Christmas Carol* and *Martin Chuzzlewit*.

Students can best understand antisemitism when they go beyond Dickens's writing and connect it with popular culture in a more in-depth exploration, one that includes historical context, images, film, Internet research, guest speakers—and graphic novels. A multimodal approach, which is developed not only by text but also in images, pictures, and film, is especially enriching and synergistic in the investigation of racism. Learning to examine racist pictorial representations carefully can help students to critique the images invoked by a close reading of the written text.

Recently, we led a group of English majors, in their final course before student teaching, in a close examination of *Oliver Twist*, the graphic novel *Fagin the Jew*, and several film versions of the story. We began by asking what the students knew about Jewish stereotypes and their perceptions of Jewish people. These future teachers seemed to have had little contact with Jewish people and to know little about antisemitism and its history. One student responded,

> I have never had a specific perception of Jewish people. My experience with Jewish people and Jewish faith is through the media and a couple of friends in school, but those few resources are obviously not enough for me to be considered truly educated on the topic.

Another commented,

> Well, during my K–12 years, I had one Jewish student in my classes that I can remember. In elementary school, this meant that we had a holiday party where we learned about each holiday in December, Hanukkah as well as Christmas. Right now, one of my closest friends is Jewish and we actually have a running joke about another friend of ours who doesn't understand why she doesn't celebrate Christmas.

Several future teachers were familiar with the stereotype that Jews are, as one student put it, "money hungry and crooked."

The jumping-off point for their examination of the Jewish stereotype was a close look at clips portraying Fagin from three different film versions of *Oliver Twist*. Rather than simply reading the novel and viewing one film version, this class undertook a more focused and, we believe, more meaningful analysis. Studying the depictions in film was an excellent way to prepare students to read the graphic novel, which uses both novelistic and filmic techniques. From each film, we closely examined the same scene: the first presentation of Fagin, when Oliver is taken to his "lair." By comparing the same scene as depicted by different directors and actors, we were able to go deeply into the content of the presentation and the cinematographic techniques. We could see how the filmmakers used lighting, clothing, speech and accent, physical features, hair, and body movements to create their representations of Fagin. Since students had also just read the corresponding passage from Dickens, we could examine the way in which each film altered or embellished Dickens's description and dialogue. Each film was fascinating in its own way and helped us develop an understanding of antisemitism in the context of Dickens's writing. All of the films would be good choices for teachers exploring this novel. (Different versions are readily available; we were able to borrow all of the films from a local library, and four versions were at the local video store.)

The first version was a fascinating black-and-white portrayal of Fagin by the actor Alec Guinness in a film directed by David Lean in 1948. Students may well be familiar with Guinness from his role as Obiwan Kenobi, the loving mentor of the lost boy Luke Skywalker in the original *Star Wars*. (Guinness also appears in *The Empire Strikes Back* and *Return of the Jedi*.) As Fagin, Guinness is a different mentor altogether—his powerful, disturbing, and well-acted portrayal of Fagin draws on antisemitic imagery (including the original illustrations to Dickens's novel by George Cruickshank) to create a frightening, even monstrous representation of a Jew who steals Christian boys. His nose is elongated; he uses stereotypical speech patterns and Yiddish phrases; he has a long, forked beard and enormous, deeply shadowed eyebrows (see Figure 8.3). Although Alec Guinness's Fagin can, at moments, seem sympathetic, even fatherly, this sympathy is clearly a mask to manipulate the boys. The lighting emphasizes the dinginess of the poverty and the slum areas, reminiscent of common woodcuts, lithographs, and black-and-white drawings depicting Jews and poverty in the nineteenth century.

The 1968 musical film *Oliver!* stars Ron Moody as a more sympathetic Fagin. Here he is a crook, but a happy, singing, dancing crook. It is Bill Sykes who becomes the more frightening embodiment of evil. Yet the Jewish stereotype still remains. Fagin has a large nose; a slouched, hunched way of walking; a sly, sneakiness that is sometimes hidden behind a falsely attractive exterior. If this Fagin is less immediately menacing, the stereotype is, perhaps, all the more frightening because here "the Jew" is deceptive, dangerous, a menace that the innocent or ill-informed might not fully recognize. A Fagin of this kind is consistent with the representation of Jews as tricky and conspiratorial.

The last film clip we studied was from a 1997 made-for-television Disney version of *Oliver Twist*. Here, Elijah Wood plays the artful dodger, and Richard Dreyfus is Fagin. This movie plays down the ominous poverty and dark lighting of earlier versions, and Richard Dreyfus's Fagin is more playful, yet the deceptiveness and the frightening possibilities of the character are still present. Costume and makeup reproduce the Jewish stereotype, reminiscent of the 1948 Alec Guinness version, with extended nose and all. Closely comparing the scenes in the

Figure 8.3. Alec Guinness as Fagin.

three film versions and in Dickens's novel led to rich class discussion about directorial choices and the difficulty of trying to separate Jewish stereotypes from this profoundly antisemitic story. One student pointed out,

> In *Oliver Twist* Dickens depicts Fagin as a thief and a cheater and refers repeated[ly] to him as "the Jew." Dickens identifies his behaviors with his culture instead of his own personal decisions.

In viewing the films, we were shocked to see that—after the Holocaust, after the antiracist movements of the 1960s, and even into our own time—these overtly racist films were still being produced, and, even more disturbing, that the racist elements of the original novel are still accepted. Where in the modern versions of *Oliver Twist* are the questions about the historical representation of Jews? How might the story be told, if it must be told, in a way that would reveal stereotypes rather than reinforce them?

Studying the text and the films prepared the class for Will Eisner's graphic novel *Fagin the Jew*, which attempts precisely to reveal and explore the Fagin stereotype. Eisner reframes the *Oliver Twist* story, creating a new background for Fagin that is intended to make his behavior in the novel more understandable. The first third of *Fagin the Jew* is a back story that shows how prejudice and mistreatment of Fagin led to his life of crime. Fagin arrives in England as a child fleeing persecution in central Europe. Due to the poverty of central European Jews in London, Fagin is forced to sell pins and buttons on the street. His father, manifesting unexplained criminal tendencies, teaches the boy how to cheat middle-class Englishmen by replacing real coins with fake ones. After describing Fagin's harsh upbringing, including a failed romance and a trip abroad, the rest of the graphic novel retells the *Oliver Twist* story. The book is structured as a plea to Dickens from Fagin before he is to be hanged, and there is an epilogue in which Oliver, now grown up, discovers that Fagin should actually have inherited a fortune. The illustrations of *Fagin the Jew* are in browns and sepias, and Fagin's image is considerably softened, both in the drawings and the narrative. For all of their appeal, graphic novels are deceptively simple, and a careful reading involves understanding their textual and filmic qualities. Angles and perspectives of the illustrations—as well as lighting, cutaway, and transition "shots"—shape the way that the graphic text is read and viewed. In *Fagin the Jew*, Eisner increases the complexity of the genre with extensive framing of the tale's narration, as well as a historical epilogue commenting on antisemitic texts and images. All of these dimensions are of potential interest to students and help them to reexamine Dickens's text. Original nineteenth-century illustrations (reprinted in this essay), as well as the more contemporary films and still photographs that we examined, are excellent sources for student projects. Some students asked how the images of the graphic novel compared with the other illustrations.

On the cover of *Fagin the Jew*, for instance, Fagin seems more like an avuncular protector of children than the threatening figure described later in the text. As one student put it, "Fagin was presented as a caring individual that wished to take Oliver in and make sure that he was fed and taken care of." *Fagin the Jew* includes a foreword and an epilogue in which Eisner explains his attempt to counter antisemitic imagery in popular culture. Eisner describes how Dickens portrayed Jews as criminals and includes some contemporary prints from the period (see Figure 8.4) that clearly show the presence of the kind of Jewish stereotype that Dickens was reproducing in his novel.

Figure 8.4. From the cover of *Fagin the Jew* by Will Eisner.

The graphic novel *Fagin the Jew* is thus an important resource for teachers and students seeking to think critically about the stereotyping of Jews in Dickens's *Oliver Twist*. Foregrounding Fagin as a character who is a member of a Jewish community, at least as a child, brings to the reader's attention questions about the historical experience of Jewish people as a group, an experience that Dickens, by merely accepting the stereotype, appears to have no interest in. Telling the story from Fagin's point of view invites students to reconsider the antisemitic narrative. Eisner's illustrations represent one extreme of the graphic novel genre, a move toward realism. Thus, they are very different from the animal fable characterizations of Spiegelman's *Maus* or the sophisticated comic book superheroes of Moore and Gibbons's *Watchmen*. Eisner's graphic novel explicitly attempts to talk back to previous cartoonish representations of Jews, providing a counterpoint to the illustrations by George Cruickshank from the original text of *Oliver Twist* and to the images in many of the stereotyped films. In the graphic novel, Fagin at least looks like a real person, not a racist caricature. The information Eisner provides about Jews in England in the nineteenth century is valuable and provides a jumping-off point for further investigation. The graphic novel format as Eisner develops it can be effective with a wide range of readers, including high school students.

Yet, in many ways, *Fagin the Jew* is also unsatisfying. Eisner doesn't go far enough in criticizing the stereotypes and the antisemitic story line of Dickens's novel. Although we learn about the poverty of the central European Jewish community in London, we are still led to believe that dishonesty, immorality, and thievery were the common response of nineteenth-century Jews. Although Eisner provides some explanation for Fagin's behavior, he does not fully challenge Dickens's fundamental racist depiction, nor does he undo the repetition of the antisemitic plot itself, in which Christian children are menaced by immoral Jews. While presumably attempting to inject historical accuracy, Eisner continues and even elaborates on Dickens's use of unlikely coincidence, romantic happenstance, and twists of fate, thus making it difficult to sort out historical context or to understand the behavior of characters. For us, even Eisner's graphic novel raises the question: Is retelling the *Oliver Twist* story, even in this somewhat critical and more attractive version, an adequate response to the fundamentally antisemitic characterization and story line of the original novel? Rather than being a satisfying and radical break from what has come before it, the question becomes whether the graphic novel is still too closely tied to previous narrative forms and imagery. These powerful questions will only arise in a complete cultural study that includes the graphic novel in student dialogues about the genres and cultural patterns that *Fagin the Jew* extends and criticizes.

Nonetheless, after studying *Fagin the Jew*, the future teachers in the class were excited about using graphic novels in the classroom. One aspiring teacher pointed out:

> Some students are visual learners whereas others prefer plain reading. By bringing in a comic book or graphic novel you get the best of both worlds. I never really used to appreciate comics, but now I would love to use them in a thoughtful, integrative lesson plan.

Taken together, film, images, and graphic novels, along with traditional literary works, were empowering for students and led not only to a more meaningful reading of the literary works, but also to a deeper understanding of the historical and cultural context, all of which was necessary to appreciating the full implications of the graphic novel genre.

Of course, antisemitism extends past the nineteenth and into the twentieth and twenty-first centuries. After reading Dickens (or Chaucer or Shakespeare), it is also valuable for students to examine the texts and images of more modern antisemitism, of the kind directly associated with the Holocaust and contemporary hate crimes. Allen Webb's students read "The Nazification of Culture," "The Control of Press, Radio, Films," and "Education in the Third Reich" (from *The Rise and Fall of the Third Reich* by William Shirer, pp. 241–56) to examine how Hitler controlled culture and education. It would also be useful to look at some of the specific imagery of the period and compare it with historical representations, such as those of Fagin, to help students see more clearly the dangers of antisemitism and consider the way propaganda works, inside or outside of literature.

The depiction in Figure 8.5, for example, is from a book for children called *The Poisoned Mushroom* (1938), written by Julius Streicher, a Nazi publisher who was tried and executed for crimes against humanity at Nuremberg. The image illustrates an episode entitled "What Hans and Else experienced with a stranger." The caption under the picture is "Here, little boy, you can have something real sweet. But then, you must both go with me." The episode about Hans and Else concludes with the following saying, which Hans's mother requires him to memorize:

> A devil goes through the land,
> It's the Jew, well-known to us
> as a murderer of peoples,
> a race defiler, a child's horror in all lands!
> Corrupting our youth
> stands him in good stead.

Figure 8.5. From *The Poisoned Mushroom.*

He wants all peoples dead.
Stay away from every Jew,
and happiness will come to you.

How far, we ask, is this Nazi story, depiction, and poetry from the narrative, characterization, and images of *Oliver Twist*?

In our view, it is essential to connect the study of the Holocaust with an examination of the cultural artifacts that created the moral and intellectual climate, the racism and antisemitism, that allowed the Holocaust to take place. Connecting the great artists of English literature to this history is part of our responsibility as teachers of English.

The frightening but bitter truth is that antisemitism exists in the world today in many forms, including antisemitic hate groups such as the neo-Nazis and Aryan supremacy groups, global banking and media conspiracy theories targeting Jews, racist caricatures of Israeli politicians, "traditional Jewish jokes" (i.e., insults), and the continuing desecration of Jewish synagogues and cemeteries. The continued reproduction and popularity of *Oliver Twist* needs to be considered in this context. Reading Dickens, Chaucer, and Shakespeare and discussing their works through a cultural studies perspective that connects their writing with historical events and issues in the present helps students become more sophisticated readers and thinkers and better citizens. Some of the representations are complex, and their relationship with antisemitic discourse may be ambiguous. Yet teaching the works with problematic representations of Jews without addressing antisemitism risks making the classroom a forum to reproduce and disseminate racist ideas.

We end this essay with another picture (see Figure 8.6) of orphaned children at risk, not fictional children this time, but once living beings, such as Anne Frank herself and the many other victims and survivors of antisemitic persecution whose lives were lost or devastated by racist ideology. Consider how this picture is a reversal of gaze from *The Poisoned Mushroom* and *Oliver Twist*. We hope such a picture suggests the importance of teachers and students investigating antisemitism and exploring the disturbing implications of *Oliver Twist* and similar works.

Recommended Resources

The Electronic Canterbury Tales, Prioress Tale page, has links to original and modern translations of the tale, background sources, additional medieval antisemitic legends and scholarly resources. http://hosting.uaa.alaska.edu/afdtk/ect_prioress.htm

"Shakespeare and Anti-Semitism: The Question of Shylock" has information about the history of Jews in England. http://www.geocities.com/Athens/Acropolis/7221/

Figure 8.6. Jewish children orphaned in the Holocaust.

The Rise and Fall of the Third Reich by William Shirer offers a readable, comprehensive history of the Nazi regime written by an American correspondent who lived in Germany in the 1930s. Students might focus on the following sections: "The Nazification of Culture," "The Control of Press, Radio, Films," and "Education in the Third Reich" (pp. 241–56).

Todd Strasser's novel, *The Wave: The Classroom Experiment That Went Too Far*, and the film made from it demonstrate to American students that fascism can happen in the United States in a school like theirs.

"Anne Frank Remembered" is a documentary film with interviews of Anne's friends, family, and protectors to depict her life before hiding, in the annex, her capture, the Auschwitz camp, and her death in Bergen-Belsen.

Art Spiegelman's *Maus I and II* is a Pulitzer Prize-winning exploration of the experience of a survivor and his son, written in a graphic novel format.

The United States Holocaust Memorial Museum has extensive materials for teachers and students. http://www.ushmm.org/

Oliver Twist in Film

- *Oliver Twist* (1909 short, J. Stuart Blackton) Production Co: Vitagraph Company of America (**not available for sale)
- *Oliver Twist* (1912/I) Distributor: States Rights Independent Exchanges (**not for sale, first known film, 4/5 of the original reels have been recovered)
- *Oliver!* (1968, Carol Reed) Distributor: Columbia Pictures
- *Oliver Twist* (1948, David Lean) Distributor: Eagle-Lion Films, Inc.
- *Oliver & Company* (1988, George Scribner) (cartoon) Distributor: Buena Vista Pictures
- *Oliver Twist* (1997 television movie, Tony Bill) Distributor: Buena Vista Television
- *Oliver Twist* (1999 television mini-series, Renny Rye) Distributor: Public Broadcasting Service (PBS)
- *Oliver Twist* (2005, Roman Polanski) Distributor: Sony Pictures Entertainment

Notes

1. The term *Antisemitismus* was first used in German in 1879 by Wilhelm Marr, meaning *Judenhass* or *Jew-hatred*. The term is confusing, since "Semitic" refers not only to Jews, but other Middle Eastern people, including Arabs. Even the notion of an ethnic or racial identity such as "Semitic peoples" is in question. Thus, by spelling the term as "antisemitism," we refer specifically to Jewish people and intend to avoid the implicit assumption in the hyphen and capital letter of the accepted spelling "anti-Semitism" that "Semitic" is racially meaningingful.

2. Gelber, Mark. (1979)."Teaching 'Literary Anti-Semitism': Dickens' *Oliver Twist* and Freytag's *Soll und Haben*." *Comparative Literature Studies, 16*(1), p. 4.

3. See Carey-Webb, 2001, pp. 13–32.

References

Bridger, D. (1976). *The new Jewish encyclopedia*. New York: Behrman House.

Carey-Webb, A. (2001). *Literature and lives: A response-based, cultural studies approach to teaching English*. Urbana, IL: NCTE.

de Gobineau, A. (1999). *The inequality of the human races*. New York: H. Fertig.

Dickens, C. (2003). *Oliver Twist*. New York: Penguin.

Eisner, W. (2003). *Fagin the Jew*. New York: Doubleday.

Hiemer, E. (1938). *Der Giftpilz* [The poisoned mushroom]. Retrieved April 5, 2005, from http://www.calvin.edu/academic/cas/gpa/thumb.htm

Shirer, W. (1990). *The rise and fall of the Third Reich*. New York: Simon & Schuster.

9 Using Graphic Novels, Anime, and the Internet in an Urban High School

Nancy Frey and Douglas Fisher
San Diego State University

Adolescents who struggle with reading and writing are often grouped in "remedial" classes and spend countless hours with worksheets and tutoring with paraprofessionals. The focus of many intervention programs is basic skills, such as decoding. But as Gallego and Hollingsworth (2000) remind us, these intervention programs fail to recognize the multiple literacies that the students possess. Using popular culture builds on students' multiple literacies (Alvermann, Moon, & Hagood, 1999), as we found when we employed alternative genres such as graphic novels, manga, and anime. Students used these and other forms of popular culture, including the Internet and teen magazines, to enhance their creation of a photo essay.

Meet the Class

We were intrigued by the status of graphic novels among adolescents. We hoped this hidden literacy might allow us to create lessons in reading and writing that addressed the multiple literacies our students possessed and needed to develop. Hoover High School, in the most densely populated and poorest community in San Diego, is notable in its diversity—over thirty languages are spoken by 2,200 students, who all qualify for the federal free or reduced lunch program. The thirty-two students in our class were ninth graders enrolled in a ninety-minute class designed for struggling readers and writers. Seventy-two percent of the thirty-two students were English-language learners who had not yet developed proficiency in English. Their average reading level was 5.4

This essay is a revised version of a previously published essay: Frey, N., & Fisher, D. (2004). Using graphic novels, anime, and the Internet in an urban high school. *English Journal, 93*(3), 19–25. Copyright © 2004 by the National Council of Teachers of English.

on the Gates-MacGinitie assessment (2000). Of the thirty-two, twenty-four were Latino/Latina, four were Asian American, three were African American, and one was White.

As university teacher-educators working in a partnership with a large urban high school, we were interested in enhancing literacy acquisition for adolescents from diverse backgrounds. This article discusses our experiences teaching a ninth-grade writing course that emphasized the use of popular culture as a vehicle for developing students' writing skills.

Scaffolding Instruction: Using Graphic Novels as Writing Prompts

We had observed students actively engaged with anime and manga materials (see sidebar), although not as part of sanctioned school activities. Evidence of their interest usually appeared in the margins of their writer's notebook pages, on the covers of assignment folders, and in the sheaves of drawings they squirreled away in their backpacks. When we attempted to strike up conversations about these works, students seemed reluctant to discuss them (perhaps because it would disclose a literary form belonging to their generation, not ours). When we explored graphic novels in local bookstores, we found both positive elements and serious drawbacks to our incorporating this material into writing instruction. A barrier for school use is the predominance of violence and sexual images in many graphic novels. On the other hand, the limited amount and level of the text would allow students to read and respond to complex messages and text combinations that better matched their reading levels.

A Manga Primer

The manga genre is more widespread in Japan than in Western countries and dates back to the early part of the twentieth century. Japanese manga, rendered in black and white and printed on newsprint, are read by children and adults and include many topics, although science fiction "mechas" (robots) dominate the field. The topics are surprisingly similar to those in Western young adult fiction. A large portion of the market is "shojo," comic books designed to appeal to girls. On the other hand, "shonen" manga are designed primarily for boys and usually consist of action stories. However, unlike the broad range of genres available in Japan, the stream of manga reaching Western shores appears to be skewed toward violent and sexu-

Continued

> ally graphic titles (called "hentai," or "perverse") and does not reflect the wide range of quality available. Many manga are published in serial form and together can be up to 750 pages.

We continued to look for the appropriate graphic novel materials, and our persistence finally paid off when we discovered the works of Will Eisner, one of the original developers of the graphic novel in the West. Eisner's material would work in our classroom—his subject matter was primarily about urban life and therefore addressed topics familiar to our students, the stories were short (often 1–3 pages), and his artistic style was quite different from the anime images we had seen before in the students' possession. This last consideration was important because we did not want to co-opt something that belonged to the students. Rather, we chose to tap into their understanding of texts that rely as much on a visual vocabulary as a written one. Eisner's *New York: The Big City* (1986) was especially useful in our classroom because it was divided into short, independent chapters.

We began with "Hydrant" as a shared reading. Each student had a copy of the wordless six-panel story (see Figure 9.1) that tells the tale of a woman living in a tenement without running water. She must carry pails of water filled at the fire hydrant outside her building up flights of stairs to prepare a bottle for her baby. As she feeds the baby, she gazes solemnly at some tropical landscape photographs stuck into the frame of a mirror. One photograph stands out—a woman carrying buckets of water on a yoke balanced across her shoulders. Using a think-aloud technique (Oster, 2001, p. 65), we began "reading" the story while pointing out techniques the artist used to convey meaning.

We also brainstormed to produce descriptive vocabulary that could be used to capture the drama. We did not discuss the ending, which was left up to the imaginations of the student writers.

Students then wrote the story using words. They took various perspectives, but most of them focused on the lost promise of a better life in a new land. Frederico's first draft, "Escaping Jamaica," represents a fairly traditional retelling of the story (all student work is presented as written):

> The home of opportunity is what they call the US. As this Jamaican lady goes to get water from a fire hydrant she thinks, "I was beter off at home." Her neighborhood is destroyed and her house looks like it may colaps on her and her baby. She carries the water the stories up just to feed her son. "Come on baby," she said,

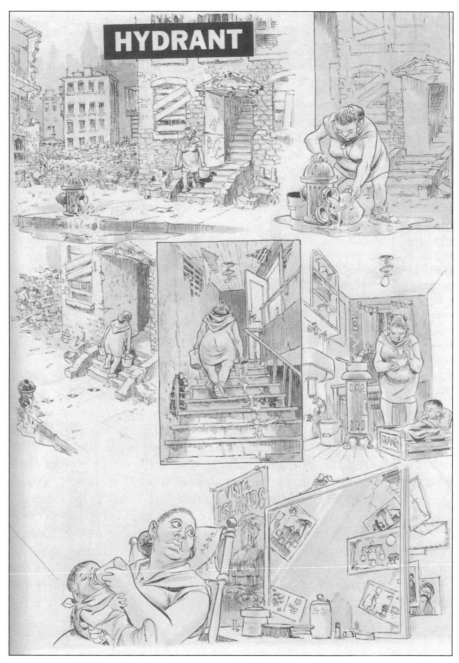

Figure 9.1. The wordless story "Hydrant" tests students' inferencing skills and offers writing opportunities.

"food is almost ready." As she feeds her son she looks at the photographs she took back home and said, "I thought this was the
land of oportunities."

We were pleased that Frederico used dialogue to propel the story and
provide insight into the character. Previous lessons had emphasized
dialogue construction and the attendant punctuation difficulties.
Frederico's draft suggests that he had mastered the use of these meaning markers, even breaking a sentence in two ("'Come on baby,' she said,
'food is almost ready.'") to increase the tension in this simple statement.

Sanjit, a student whose family had emigrated from Thailand several years ago, was facing great difficulty in his life. A week after he
wrote the following story, he told us that his family had been served an
eviction notice for having too many people living together. He entitled
his story "Irony":

Life is miserable, isn't it? Freedom and happiness . . . that's what
they promise in America, isn't it? This is what I thought when I
was still living in the islands, but "boy" was I in for it. I think this
is what they call poor in America. Who would have ever imagined that I have to go through such labor just to feed my son? Ha
Ha. Looks like I can't escape but at least my homeland bring some
happiness into my life.

Sanjit's story differed from the ending that Frederico and other students
chose. He regarded the photographs on the mirror as a comfort for the
protagonist, unlike Frederico's interpretation of the photos as reflect-
ing the decline in the quality of the woman's life.

Encouraged by the student responses, we were determined to
provide more opportunities for the use of graphic novel excerpts as a
means for writing. Over the next two weeks, we used chapters from
various works by Eisner, as well as excerpts from other graphic novels
(see the sidebar). We followed a similar lesson plan format each time:
Use the text as a shared reading, instruct using a think-aloud strategy,
and discuss word choice and vocabulary as devices to give power to
the writer's message. Visual stories allowed students to discuss how the
authors conveyed mood and tone through images. We could then discuss techniques for doing so through words.

Graphic Novels and Picture Books Used as Writing Prompts

Bey, Elihu. Still I Rise: A Cartoon History of African Americans. *New York: W.
    W. Norton, 1997. A graphic novel depicting the extensive history of African
    Americans from the Middle Passage to the 1990s.*

Charlip, Remy. Fortunately. *New York: Scott Foresman, 1993. A picture book about a boy's attempt to attend a birthday party that alternates between "fortunately" and "unfortunately."*

Collins, Max Allen, and Richard Rayner. Road to Perdition. *New York: Paradox, 1998. A groundbreaking graphic novel of a hit man for the Irish American mob in the 1930s who must protect his young son from the people he works for.*

David, Lawrence. Beetle Boy. *New York: Dragonfly, 1999. This picture book is inspired by Kafka (with a happy ending) and recounts a day in the life of Gregory, a young boy who awakes to find he has become a beetle.*

Eisner, Will. New York: The Big City. *Princeton, WI: Kitchen Sink Press, 1986. The grandfather of Western graphic novels portrays the trials and tribulations of his fellow New Yorkers.*

Eisner, Will. City People Notebook. *Princeton, WI: Kitchen Sink Press, 1989. Eisner is continually inspired by the small details of urban dwelling in this insightful graphic novel.*

Eisner, Will, P. Craig Russell, John McCrae, Eric Powell, Jon J. Muth, et al. 9-11: Artists Respond, *Volume 1. Dark Horse Comics, 2002. Notable comic book artists from around the world offer their impressions of the tragedy of 9/11 and the struggle of survivors, rescue workers, and citizens to understand how the world changed.*

Giardino, Vittorio, and Joe Johnson [Trans.] A Jew in Communist Prague: 2, Adolescence. *New York: NBM, 1997. The second of a three-part epic graphic novel follows Jonas as he tries to support his family after his father is imprisoned.*

Kafka, Franz and Peter Kuper. Give It Up! and Other Short Stories by Kafka. *New York: NBM, 1999. Kuper illustrates nine short stories by Kafka in this graphic novel that sends a powerful psychological message of dark humor in the midst of despair.*

Smith, Charles R., Jr. (2001). Loki and Alex: The Adventures of a Dog and His Best Friend. *New York: Dutton, 2001. A photographic essay that alternates perspectives between a boy and his dog as they interpret common situations very differently.*

Wegman, William. My Town. *New York: Hyperion, 1998. The dogs are at it again, and this time they must write a school report, even though they would rather use photographs to illustrate the assignment.*

Wegman, William. Surprise Party. *New York: Hyperion, 2000. Wegman's pet Weimaraners star in this campy send-up of a surprise party for one of the dogs.*

Wegman, William, Carole Kismaric, and Marvin Heiferman. Little Red Riding Hood. *New York: Hyperion, 1999. An unorthodox retelling of the familiar fairy tale that stars the author's famous dogs.*

Wiesner, David. Tuesday. *New York: Clarion, 1991. This wordless picture book imaginatively portrays a mysterious Tuesday night when frogs fly and hijinks ensue.*

When we noticed that students overused the word *said* in their dialogues, we presented a lesson called "Said is dead" (Peterson, 1996, p. 33) to introduce more creative ways to indicate speech. Another lesson on shades of meaning in words was connected to an episode depicting the thirteen-year-old protagonist's search for a job to support his hungry family in Vittorio Giardino's "A Jew in Communist Prague." Using the "shades of meaning" metaphor (suggested by paint-chip cards that had been donated by a local home improvement store), students selected and arranged a continuum of five words related to a topic (Goodman, 2003, p. 79). Students consulted dictionaries and thesauri to complete the cards and then used some of the words in their writing. For example, Yesenia's card looked like this:

Shades of Meaning:
HUNGRY
Fasting
Hungry
Ravenous
Famished
Starving

These words apparently resonated with Yesenia, who had arrived two years earlier from Mexico, and she applied them in a way that surprised us. Rather than write on the assigned story about the boy seeking a job, she incorporated these words into a version of her "Hydrant" story, entitled "A Depres Women":

> On a regular day in a rusty town, this women came out from a house to get water. The woman looked very tier. She got the water and go up stairs to her famished baby. The hallway looked all ruined and as she entered the room; the ravenous baby waiting for her. When the bottle was ready she sat down with the baby and looked at the mirror. Pictures of where she used to live were in her mind; she tought, "It would be better if I still lived in my island." She felt depres because she couldn't do anything to help herself or her starving baby.

Although there were numerous spelling and syntactic errors, common among writers working in a second language, we were heartened to see that she had engaged in the act of revision in the authentic way that writers revise—not as a step in a process, but because she had a new idea to explore within an existing piece.

Students also needed to learn how to convey multiple ideas efficiently, in one or two sentences. We taught many rounds of Triple Sentence Sessions (Fearn and Farnan, 2001, p. 147). In this brief writing exercise, the teacher introduces three ideas (not words) in succession for students to turn into a cohesive writing passage. We brainstormed to produce words and phrases to represent each idea. Students then wrote a sentence containing the idea, using words they had heard in the discussion or others they recalled. It is important to note that only one idea unit was presented at a time so that students could not plan the combination of their sentences in advance. Once we began with the idea of teenager, Sanjit wrote, "The youth looked down at his siblings." The next idea was a meal, and he wrote, "The youth looked down at his siblings. His eyes focused on their lunch." The final idea was a crime, so he now wrote, "The youth looked down at his siblings then focused his eyes on their lunch. Quickly, he snatched the lunches away." Based on the same three ideas, Tynessia wrote, "Young people today are oppressed by the lack of quality school lunches. It is a crime that the school gets paid to serve what they serve."

We began to see more evidence of complex sentences and multiple ideas in their work. Five-minute timed-writing samples over the course of this unit bore this out; the mean sentence length in the class increased from 11.2 to 12.89 during the span of this four-week unit. As student confidence grew, we presented only the beginning of a chapter and asked students to construct the ending. Eisner's chapter "Art" opens with two young males lurking around a dark rail yard, spray paint cans in hand. They scale a fence and paint the word *Chico* in huge letters across the side of a subway train. We ended the story there and invited students to create the ending. We discussed the use of dialogue, vocabulary, and multiple ideas to make their piece more compelling. Daisha wrote a first draft called "It Would Have Been Nice to Ask":

> My brother and his friend was walking to the store. His friend gave him an incentive to go tag the subway, so they jumped the fence and walked over there. See, my brother is the kind of guy that when someone tells him to do something he will do it. Well, as they got the spray paint ready they was talking about their friends looking up to them for doing this. So they started to do their little "art" when the police caught them. They was scared and was saying, "Please don't tell our parents!" The officer said, "we have to, son." The police officer then said, "We're going to let you off with a warning but next time it's all over." Officer Brown then surprised them both. "Ya'll wouldn't have got in trouble because the owner likes kind of stuff."

Daisha employed an effective literary device by making the meaning of the title clear only at end of the passage. This piece required some editing, especially regarding the conventions of grammar. However, the revised piece did not differ from the original in its tone or surprise ending.

The Culminating Project: Photo Essays as Popular Culture

Using graphic novels to scaffold writing instruction helped students practice the craft of writing and gain the necessary skills to become competent readers. After several weeks of using graphic novel excerpts, we introduced the culminating project—a photo essay. This assignment was designed to extend our creative writing instruction. It was not to be autobiographical. We hoped that students' multiple experiences of closely examining visual imagery as a means of telling a story had prepared them for this project. We distributed disposable cameras to the students and outlined general rules for using them in school. The first frame was used to photograph the writer for later use in an "about the author" segment on the inside of the back cover.

We also modeled teacher-constructed photo essays and described our creative process in writing the text. Using photographs from a formal party, we described a fanciful and completely fictitious event. A teacher candidate assigned to our classroom also modeled a story. Using black-and-white images from a book on psychological images in therapy, she wrote a five-part serial on a mysterious house and its ghostly inhabitants. We later discovered that this piece inspired one of our students to use a similar technique.

We encouraged students to apply alternative texts and nontraditional information sources to their work. They had access to three computers with Internet connections, and we scheduled several class periods in the school's computer lab so that students could use images from Web sites to enhance their work. In addition, we discussed how the text and illustrations work together to tell a story in several picture books (see the box on pages 136–37). The books had fantasy themes or storylines that were clearly fictitious in nature, because the students' photo essays were to be of a similar genre. For example, we used Lawrence David's *Beetle Boy* for its innovative retelling of Franz Kafka's novella *Metamorphosis* and as a link to a graphic novel of Kafka's works interpreted by Peter Kuper that we had viewed earlier in the unit. William Wegman's fairy tales using Weimaraner dogs to portray the characters were well received. Wordless picture books, such as *Tuesday* by David Wiesner, linked to the graphic novel excerpts we had previously read. Many of the devices used in these picture books appeared in student work.

After the film was developed, students began constructing a cohesive story. We required that at least fifteen images with supporting text be included in the photo essay. We conferred orally with students as they constructed their stories because we have found that talking through the assignment with students in the initial stages of a project can be particularly valuable to English-language learners and to other students who struggle with writing. Saying their ideas out loud seems to free them to use words without the self-editing that poor spellers often perform (Lapp & Flood, 1993, p. 256). In some cases, we scribed important words and phrases for later student use as a modified version of a Language Experience Approach (Fisher & Frey, 2003, p. 398). We later read the drafts and supported the revisions. In the final stages, students engaged in peer editing. Then they mounted the images and text on sheets of construction paper that had been assembled using the school's binding machine.

The resulting works were a fascinating lens on popular culture and its artifacts in adolescent writing. All of the thirty-two students completed the project and, although most used their photographs to illustrate their essays, some used nontraditional techniques. Two students, both accomplished artists, used original anime art exclusively, and a third student used panels from graphic novels we had read in class to complement his photographs. A member of a punk band called "Verbal Diarrhea" illustrated his photo essay of the band hitting it big by cutting the photographs and then completing the images with original art for a collage effect.

Other students were inspired by writing that they had seen before in unit lessons. Juanita's story, "The Last Goodbye," employed the psychological thriller theme used in the photo essay that had been modeled by the teacher candidate. Juanita clipped images from teen magazines to illustrate the story using panels. An excerpt of the opening of her essay read as follows:

> Last summer Jane and her mom Tonia went to visit her grandfather in L.A. Her grandfather liked writing love stories and sad stories in the basement of his house. . . . The next day Jane asked her grandfather, "Who is the lady in the picture?" He sat her on his lap and sighed, "That was the love of my life, but now she is gone." They both just sat quietly.

Many students used Eisner's urban life themes in their writing. Arturo's "A Tragic Hit on Cinco de Mayo" began:

> San Luis Obispo was silent. Violence was nowhere to be found. Peace was unique and rich and friendliness was everywhere. It was the day of Cinco de Mayo. A party was to take place and the food was prepared by hand so it would be fresh. People were happy and had big smiles. Kids were together and parents were talking to each other.

Soon after, an unknown gunman opens fire on the crowd, and Jack, the protagonist, pursues the perpetrator into a nearby wooded area. However, he is torn about whether to give chase or remain behind to tend to the dead and wounded:

> . . . Jack was in shock from what he had seen. He was scared of what might happen if he left the town now that death had taken place. Jack doesn't even know who killed the whole town, but he will avenge all of the death he has seen.

Several students wrote stories inspired by playing interactive games on the Internet. Minh described a tense battle in "The Tournament Starts Now." A humorous device in his photographs stood in contrast to the serious nature of the text—his two opponents were toddlers:

> It was my turn now (the best of the best in the house of game). As the tournament runner I must also play by the rules. As the day went by, so did the game. I lost money to two of my challengers . . . . I have tried my best, but could not beat the GoSu.

We were unfamiliar with the term *GoSu* but learned that it is a Korean gaming term that means "expert." Minh explained that to be named GoSu is the highest honor in Internet interactive games.

Overall, writing results were excellent, and we achieved many of the goals we had set. During the month, students increased their mean written sentence length. All of the essays featured dialogue to tell the story, and the storylines fulfilled the requirement of fantasy or creative writing. We were pleased to see that many writers explored more sophisticated word choice. The average length of the photo essays was 478 words, representing some of the most sustained writing these students had engaged in to this point.

Conclusions

Having begun with the idea that graphic novels were comic books at best and a waste of time at worst, we now realized the power they have for engaging students in authentic writing. These forms of popular culture provided a visual vocabulary of sorts for scaffolding writing techniques, particularly dialogue, tone, and mood.

More importantly, we resisted the temptation to focus on remedial skills instruction and instead used popular culture and the media to invite students into school literacy. The use of these forms of popular culture and media afforded us a space to provide students with instruction on the craft and mechanics of writing. Our students not only became better writers, but also better consumers of ideas and information.

References

Alvermann, D. E., Moon, J. S., & Hagood, M.C. (1999). *Popular culture in the classroom: Teaching and researching critical media literacy.* Newark, DE: International Reading Association.

Collins, M. A., & Rayner, R. (1998). *Road to perdition.* New York: Paradox.

Eisner, W. (1986). *New York: The big city.* Princeton, WI: Kitchen Sink Press.

Fearn, L., & Farnan, N. (2001). *Interactions: Teaching writing and the language arts.* New York: Houghton Mifflin.

Fisher, D., & Frey, N. (2003). Writing instruction for struggling adolescent readers: A gradual release model. *Journal of Adolescent & Adult Literacy, 46,* 396–405.

Gallego, M. A., & Hollingsworth, S. (Eds.). (2000). *What counts as literacy: Challenging the school standard.* New York: Teachers College.

Goodman, L. (2003). Shades of meaning: Relating and expanding word knowledge. In G. E. Tompkins, C. L. Blanchfield (Eds.), *Teaching vocabulary: 50 creative strategies, grades K–12* (pp. 83–86). Upper Saddle River, NJ: Prentice Hall.

Lapp, D., & Flood, J. (1993). Are there "real" writers living in your classroom? Implementing a writer-centered classroom. *The Reading Teacher, 47*, 254–58.

MacGinitie, W. H. (2000). *Gates-MacGinitie reading tests.* Itasca, IL: Riverside.

Mendes, S. (Director) (2002). *The road to perdition* [Motion picture]. United States: DreamWorks Pictures.

Oster, L. (2001). Using the think-aloud for reading instruction. *The Reading Teacher, 55*, 64–69.

Peterson, A. (1996). *The writer's workout book: 113 stretches toward better prose.* Berkeley, CA: National Writing Project.

10 *Ultimate Spider-Man* and Student-Generated Classics: Using Graphic Novels and Comics to Produce Authentic Voice and Detailed, Authentic Texts

James Bucky Carter
University of Virginia

Introduction

For the purpose of this collection, "classic texts" have been defined as the traditional or canonical literary texts commonly used in English language arts classrooms across the nation. Joan Kaywell's series (1993) *Adolescent Literature as a Complement to the Classics* helped convince teachers that there were just as many classic tales in the category of young adult literature as in the canon, and they have been receptive to that thinking. However, it would be remiss for this collection not to include a chapter that deals directly with a different type of classic text: those authentic texts created by our students. Authentic texts and the search for authentic voice in student writing get at the heart of English language arts. For the purposes of this essay, I define "authenticity" in writing as Cambourne (2002) does:

> [A]uthenticity refers to the degree to which learning activities used to promote reading resemble the kinds of reading activities and learning that occur outside the traditional, institutionalized school setting. The more an activity is like an everyday activity, the higher degree of authenticity it possesses. With respect to reading, writing and the other accoutrements of literacy, the more that an activity requires the students to engage in the kind of reading-writing-literacy behaviors that highly literate, proficient adults use to address their needs, the more authentic the activity is judged to be. (p. 38)

The following description details my endeavor to help sixth- and seventh-grade students in an "academically and intellectually gifted" class (the state label) to craft a piece of prompted fiction. The idea was to give students an assignment that would allow them to develop their own writers' voices—to "show 'n' tell" an authentic text via comic book writing and to edit that story such that the richness and fullness of their visions could translate from script to comic.

The Comic Book Show 'n' Tell

The Comic Book Show 'n' Tell is a unique spin on the writing workshop (Atwell, 1987). In the beginning of the lesson, I usually focus most on increasing the students' awareness of the importance of details in their writing. I inform students that we're going to study details and I ask them to provide me with examples. Just as they do with grammar rules, when asked for details, they often groan and spit out a list of many different kinds of details (adjectives, time markers, place markers, etc.) that they know about but have trouble applying. I then inform them that we're going to study details using comic books, but that, first, we need to know a little about how comics are put together. James Moffet says of sensory writing, "Whatever the material, it must *already* appeal to them. . . . Arbitrariness . . . is the enemy" (1992, p. 32). My experience has shown me that most sixth- and seventh-graders still find comics appealing. Figure 10.1 illustrates some of the terms that I share with my students, including elements of comic art, as well as descriptions of the different people involved in comics production (Pellowski, 1995). Students are often amazed to learn how much work goes into a "simple" comic book. In this way, the lesson is a genre study as well as a writing workshop. I also explain the two major styles of scripting in comics: the Marvel way and the DC way (Haines, 1998), named after the two major comic book companies. (Students enjoy matching up their favorite heroes by company: Batman, Superman, and Wonder Woman to DC, and X-Men, Spider-Man, Daredevil, and Hulk to Marvel.) The Marvel way refers to Marvel Comics' classic 1960s "assembly line" method of production: a plot would be created and then an artist would draw the scenes based on the plot. Only after the artist had sketched out the entire issue would the writer come in and add dialogue. But DC's full-script style is now the favored method of most comic companies. Although editors still have considerable input as far as plot goes, in the DC style, the writer produces a complete script, similar to the script for a play. Once the students know about these two styles, I explain that

Writer—the person who writes the script from which the story will emerge.

Artist—the person who draws the script, usually using pencils.

Inker—the person who goes over the artist's pencil lines with ink to make them stand out.

Colorist—the person who colors the inker's and artists' work, sometimes by hand and sometimes using software.

Letterer—the person who puts the words in the right places and makes them clearly legible. (The letterer might also put in the sound effects.)

Editor—the person who looks over the stories for errors as well as helps the creative team find a direction for telling the stories.

Editor-In-Chief—the boss . . . the person everyone else tries to make happy.

Parts of a Comic Book

Script—all of the written directions for how the comic book will be put together: the dialogue for the comic.

Pages—parts in the script where the writer tells what should be on each page.

Panels—rectangles or squares where the action of the script will go.

⬭ *Word balloons*—to show where people speak.

⬭ *Thought balloons*—to show when people are thinking.

Narratory blocks—little rectangles or squares where a narrator, maybe a character from the story, shares special information with the reader.

Open panels—panels where one or more, or even all, of the sides are open to help show drama.

Splash page—a panel that usually takes up the whole page and is used to help introduce stories or give special attention to battles or particular events.

Figure 10.1. Roles in comic book production.

we'll be focusing on the full-script style, which puts most of the responsibility for storytelling on the writer.

Moffet recognizes scripting as a "flexible learning means that can very effectively teach many aspects of writing and discourse—more than teachers yet appreciate" (1992, p. 46). Since teachers still sometimes need help appreciating comics, the activity can expand the understanding of students and teachers alike. Scripting is sophisticated composition, after all, "since the writer is *simulating* real speech, making up all the roles, and making a statement *by means of* her characters"(p. 48).

Afterward, I ask the students to look at the comics I've brought in and to pay attention to everything they see (students were also asked to read a comic for homework the night before the workshop). Having the same issue for every student can help the teacher draw attention to specific decisions to be made in terms of the writing and the artwork. For my class, I was able to acquire free multiple copies of *Ultimate Spider-Man #1* (see cover in Figure 10.2) from a local comic book store.[1] This comic is a modern retelling of the Spider-Man mythos, and it closely mirrors the first *Spider-Man* movie in plot. The graphic novel *Ultimate Spider-Man Volume 1* (which collects the issue the class used in addition to six more issues) is an excellent book for classroom use. Students easily relate to teenager Peter Parker, who, ever since a radioactive spider bit him to trigger his transformation, begins to undergo changes in his attitude, behavior, and physical appearance. The typical "moody teen," he captures the essence of adolescence. His superpowered puberty (see Figure 10.3) leads him to argue more with Aunt May and Uncle Ben, his guardians; to react to social situations in odd ways; and to feel new sensations.

Furthermore, the theme of the book and the long-time Spider-Man mantra, "with great power comes great responsibility," is a strong, positive message to convey to children who are quite literally on the cusp of adulthood. Indeed, *Ultimate Spider-Man Volume 1* is a bildungsroman. Peter Parker lets a criminal escape instead of using his new powers to stop him, and the thief murders Peter's uncle soon thereafter. Like many characters in young adult fantasy and science fiction literature (e.g., *The Giver*, *Ender's Game*, *Eva*), Peter sees that he is unique, but he also learns that being uniquely gifted comes with its own set of baggage. In this regard, I think that students who have been labeled "gifted" might share even deeper connections to the text than some others might.

It Begins!

Once we have studied *Ultimate Spider-Man #1*, the writing begins. Each student is asked to write a comic book using the full-script style, based on a purposely open-ended prompt such as "Superman Saves the Day." "Students only gain a sense of audience by writing for more than one person or group," says Vicki Spandel (2005, p. 222). As they write their scripts, students must "talk" to the initial reader (the artist) by giving directions, but also consider their general audience—the comic book fans who will read the completely drawn, inked, colored, and lettered comic. I give the students a deadline, just like a real comic writer would have, but in this case it's usually just ten minutes. Once this initial script writing is over, I explain to the students that comic book writers often fax or email their work to artists across the country or even overseas, and so they are often so busy with the next script that little communication takes place once the script is sent out.[2] Then the students exchange

Figure 10.2. Cover of *Ultimate Spider-Man #1*.

papers with classmates on the far side of the room with the understanding that no further communication is allowed. The writers now become artists and must draw comics based on the scripts in front of them. Next the artists silently return the scripts and their freshly drawn pages to the writers.

Figure 10.3. Peter Parker's superpowered puberty.

"Practical tryouts remain for all scripts the best entrance into discussion and revision," Moffet says (1992, p. 54). This scripting activity gives students a chance to craft stories of their own making with a large amount of freedom, but it challenges them to work quickly and to choose their wording accurately to get as much of their story on paper as they can in the allotted time. They need to write dialogue as well as descriptions. And they know that some of their writing will never be viewed as written text by the readers of the published product since it will end up being used as directions to their artists. As a result, they develop a sense of writing as both telling and showing and, perhaps equally important, as developing their voice simultaneously in multiple planes. They come to understand that the two types of writing do not, as is often claimed, always work independently.

What follows the initial scriptwriting is a discussion about how well the pages match the script. Artists return the scripts to their writers along with their sketched interpretations of the text. Was the artist able to "create clear images in the reader's mind" (Kirby, Kirby, & Liner, 2004, p. 124)? Initially, of course, the image is created in the artist's mind itself, but student artists have the further goal of creating a story that a new reader could follow and enjoy, or not. Invariably, one student scriptmaster proclaims that the artistic portrayal is "dead-on," but probing questions such as the following usually prompt reconsideration: Did the artist put everything in the background that you saw in your head? (Often, no background is dictated, or the artist leaves the panels mostly empty.) Did the artist get all of the colors right? (This question is especially fun if the students worked in pencil.) What about the clothing, was it the same? Was the alarm clock going off exactly like you saw it in your head?

Editing for Detail

The guided discussion gets students thinking about the mental pictures they had as they wrote. Students enjoy seeing their work come to life, but they also get a kick out of seeing just how different their visions are from the artists' representations. Details, I remind them, exist to help writers get what they see in their head into someone else's head. Then I model a script from *Cedric, The Dragon Slayer,*[3] one of my own amateur comic book writings (see Figure 10.4). On an overhead projector, I show a scripted page first and then contrast it with the artist's interpretation. We explore the written words and decide whether the artist was able to produce on paper a clear representation of what was in the writer's mind (see Figure 10.5). The class discussion addresses a number of questions: What details did the writer include? How much freedom was the artist allowed in his or her interpretation of the script? Should the writing have been more descriptive? Comparing the sample script page to the comic page highlights the formal differences between the two pages and reinforces the importance of detail in scripting. Then the students revise their scripts and give the artists another chance to "re-vision" the writer's intentions. Scripts from the revisions are much more detailed than the first drafts because students focus on getting their mental pictures more accurately drawn. I wrap up the lesson by reminding students that every sort of writing needs details and that anecdotes, examples, quotes, and various kinds of evidence are just other ways of using details in different types of writing. If possible, I also let them keep their issue of *Ultimate Spider-Man #1*.

Conclusions

The Comic Book Show 'n' Tell engages students in a writing workshop on authentic voice, editing, and details. As a result, students develop a metacognitive sense of the creative enterprise as a whole, while enjoying the opportunity to create an authentic text, a true student classic of sequential art. A little knowledge about how comics and graphic novels are produced provides an intrinsically entertaining means by which students learn to improve their written work, their sense of voice, and their ability to both tell and show their ideas to others. Very few forms of writing so eloquently engage showing and telling as does comic book scripting.

Students derive a greater respect for details and a new metacognition that may now be easily available for future writing. This is no small accomplishment. "[E]xperiments make clear that *verbalizing* and *writing* down impressions are difficult" for young children (Moffett, 1992, p. 31). In this case, the activity challenges and clarifies without being overly pedantic or lacking in context. This in-class workshop using *Ultimate Spider-Man #1* engages students in something drawn from their shared common knowledge of popular culture, their interests, and their experiences as adolescents. As Moffet explains, "sensory composing . . . is the proper way to get details into student writing" (p. 34). The Comic Book Show 'n' Tell helps students to become attuned to sensory elements in their writing and to understand that it's important to match what they see in their heads to what the readers see. It also provides an excellent opportunity for students to explore and develop the full range of their writerly voices.

Page 4
Panel 1:
Old Lady screams: There it is! There it is! I knew it! It's the At Last Dragon! Slay it, Dragon-Slayer!

Panel 2: (The dragon flies around and then settles in front of Cedric, sitting like a dog.)

Cedric then: HAHAHA! Ma'am, this is just a common floater dragon. They're all over this part of the countryside. They're harmless, like dogs.

Old Lady: Oh no, that there's the meanest, orneriest dragon they make!! He's done eaten my precious little Perty, I knows it, and come to think of it, I got a cow missin' too!!

Panel 3:
Cedric then: But he's only three feet tall! He couldn't possibly eat a cow.
(The dragon spits the chicken out at Cedric.)

Cedric then: And look at this; it's not even a chicken. It's a feather cap. He was probably just roosting in your roof for a while and . . .

Panel 4:
Tyber now: And then the Old Lady says, "If you was your daddy, boy, that dragon would be on my dinner table by now! You shame the family name, you yellow coward . . . well, I couldn't have her bad-mouth my buddy, you know.

Panel 5:
Tyber now: I'd been just standing there listening to her yak, but I was not gonna let her cuss my buddy, no way, uh-uh!

Panel 6:
(Tyber grabs the bartender's lips. Cedric and Tyber both smile at how comical the keeper looks, maybe crossing his eyes to see both of Tyber's massive fingers on his mouth.)

Tyber now: So I just leaned down there and grabbed her lips shut like this see . . .

Panel 7:
Cedric narrates: Now that did happen. The witch started to flail and mumble out muffled screams that probably could have been heard in the next village over. Better Tyber than me.

Figure 10.4. Sample script page from "Cedric's Pooped."

Notes

1. Many comic book stores are willing to work with teachers; they may have "quarter bins" where comics can be purchased for twenty-five cents each, as well as preorder supplies for the annual "Free Comic Book Day" promotion, in which companies donate comics for the exposure. Companies who preorder too many copies are often stuck with the remaining issues and are eager to unload them. I was able to procure a hundred copies of *Ultimate Spider-Man #1* and another comic as well.

Figure 10.5. An artist's rendering of the script page from "Cedric's Pooped."

2. This explanation doesn't go into the various complications in the process. Even though technology has made it easier and faster for creative teams to communicate today than in the past, it is still not uncommon for artists and writers working under massive time constraints and on multiple projects to delay communication.

3. I have written a number of scripts for OutcastStudios.com's *Cedric the Dragon Slayer*. The characters belong to the studio, not to me exclusively. The artist for the page shown is Eric Oakland, another member of the online community.

4. A version of this lesson can be found at http://www.readwritethink.org.

References

Atwell, N. (1987). In the middle: Writing, reading, and learning with adolescents. Upper Montclair, NJ: Boynton/Cook.

Cambourne, B. (2002). Holistic, integrated approaches to reading and language arts instruction: The constructivist framework of an instructional theory. In A. E. Farstrup & S. J. Samuels (Eds.), *What research has to say about reading instruction* (3rd ed., pp. 25–47). Newark, DE: International Reading Association.

Haines, L.(1998). *The writer's guide to the business of comics.* New York: Watson-Guptill.

Kaywell, J. F. (1993). *Adolescent literature as a compliment to the classics.* Norwood, MA: Christopher-Gordon Publishers.

Kirby, D., Kirby, D. L., & Liner, T. (2004). *Inside out* (3rd ed). Portsmouth, NH: Heinemann.

Moffett, J. (1992). *Active voice: A writing program across the curriculum* (2nd ed.). Portsmouth, NH: Boynton/Cook.

Pellowski, M. M. (1995). *The art of making comic books.* Minneapolis, MN: Lerner Publications Co.

Spandel, V. (2005). *Creating writers through 6-trait writing assessment and instruction* (4th ed., p. 222). Boston: Pearson/Allyn and Bacon.

Appendix: Additional Graphic Novels for the English Language Arts Classroom

I n addition to the important graphic novels discussed in the chapters, many more titles are available. The following annotated list is neither exhaustive nor definitive and should be considered only as a starting point for teachers seeking more ideas for classroom use or to expand the graphic novel section of their school libraries. No list is a substitute for an individual teacher's good judgment, and, of course, reading the texts is imperative to making informed choices. (Thanks to Doug Fisher and Nancy Frey for help in compiling this list.)

American Splendor: The Life and Times of Harvey Pekar (Harvey Pekar, 2003, Ballantine).

> These "slice of life" collected shorts evoke realism, naturalism, determinism, nihilism, and existentialism as "Everyman" Pekar shares tales from his life and the mutable philosophy it has spawned. Great for exploring modernism and postmodernism, the collection often recalls classic short stories such as Stephen Crane's "The Open Boat." Since various artists draw Pekar's stories, there is potential for exploring various visual styles as they relate to mood, tone, content, and subtext. Excerpts are recommended for middle and high school students. The entire text is recommended for high school students.

Batman: The Dark Knight Returns (Frank Miller, 1996, DC Comics).

> This book is a futuristic depiction of a world without Batman. Crime is rampant, and society is in decline. But what will happen when the Bat comes out of retirement to reclaim his city? Like *Watchmen* (also included in this list), this text pulls heavily from the popular culture of the 1980s and the fin de siècle mythos to create a dark, dystopian realism. The book is recommended for high school students.

Bone (Jeff Smith, 2004, Cartoon Books). One Volume Edition.

> This is a 1,300-page epic detailing the medieval journey of three lovable cousins, Fone Bone, Phony Bone, and Smiley Bone, as they take on a world of magic and adventure. The tale is full of symbolic and literary imagery. It is printed in black and white, but color versions of each

of the thirteen chapters can be purchased separately. The book is recommended for most grades.

A Contract with God and Other Tenement Stories (Will Eisner, 1996, DC Comics).

These four stories detail tenement life in New York City in the 1930s and express the intricacies of modern life while revealing Eisner to be a master of the graphic novel format that he helped establish for audiences in the United States. Excerpts are recommended for middle and high school students. The entire text is recommended for mature high school students.

Electric Girl: Volumes 1–3 (Michael Brennan, 2000–2005, AiT/Planet Lar).

The Electric Girl, Virginia, is born with the power to control electricity, and she is constantly nagged by an invisible, mischievous demon. She and her pet dog Blammo try to lead the lives of a normal girl and her dog in the United States, but they hardly ever succeed. Light and entertaining, these books are recommended for students in later elementary school and up.

Fantastic Four Legends. Volume 1: Unstable Molecules (James Sturm, 2003, Marvel).

This text is a cartoon biography of the "real-life" foursome who inspired the first family of superhero teams. It provides excellent potential for a cross-genre examination of biography, historical documents, film, and comics. It is recommended for middle and high school students.

Fax from Sarajevo: A Story of Survival (Joe Kubert, 1998, Dark Horse Comics).

Ervin Rustemagic tells a harrowing tale of life in Bosnia in the 1990s; his family's eventual escape is chronicled via actual faxes sent to his friend, comic book legend Joe Kubert. This book brings humanity to an ethnic and political conflict that is still often misunderstood. It is recommended for middle and high school students.

JSA: The Golden Age: A Different Look at a Different Era (James Robinson, 2005, DC).

In an alternate post-WWII reality, everybody in the United States is in love with patriot and hero Mr. America. He is later revealed to be an archvillain who has recently transferred Hitler's brain into the most powerful being to walk the Earth! Several 1940s-era superheroes must come to the rescue in this science fiction dystopia just begging to be studied alongside other dystopias such as *The Giver*, *Eva*, and *1984*. It is recommended for high school students.

King: A Comic Book Biography (Ho Che Anderson, 2005, Fantagraphics).

This unauthorized biography of Martin Luther King, Jr. uses actual history as well as the mythos surrounding the civil rights leader to detail his life from boyhood Mississippi to his death. It offers multiple perspectives on his work and influence. It is recommended for high school students.

Pedro and Me: Friendship, Loss, and What I Learned (Judd Winick, 2000, Henry Holt).

> Winick details his life before and after rooming with Pedro Zamora, an HIV-positive AIDS activist, during the third season of MTV's *The Real World*. Winick explores how Zamora challenges his views on sexuality and health issues and continues to be an inspiration long after his AIDS-related death. It is recommended for middle and high school students.

Rose (Jeff Smith and Charles Vess, 2002, Cartoon Books).

> A prequel to the Bone stories, this book reveals the history of Bone's fiesty Gran'ma Ben. A princess in her younger days, she fights to defend her kingdom from a mysterious dragon, but not without sacrifice. The book is beautifully rendered and recommended for students in most grades.

Safe Area Gorazde and *Palestine* (Joe Sacco, 2001, Fantagraphics Books).

> Both of these graphic novels explore the author's time in hot spot regions of the world and are innovative journalistic accounts of regional political conflicts. They are recommended for high school students.

The Sandman Series (Neil Gaiman, 1988–present, DC Comics).

> Amazing fantasy and allegory emerge from the mists of Gaiman's dream world, with allusions to mythology and fine literature, such as Shakespeare, deftly integrated throughout. Metaphysical mayhem, suspense, angst, and high fantasy are rarely combined so well. The series is recommended for high school students.

Still I Rise: A Cartoon History of African Americans (Roland Own Laird, 1997, W. W. Norton).

> Starting with the Jamestown colony and progressing to the twentieth century, this book chronicles the achievements of African Americans and explores their struggles and triumphs. It is recommended for students in late elementary school and up.

The Tale of One Bad Rat (Bryan Talbot, 1995, Dark Horse).

> Full of symbolic imagery and literary allusion, this book details teen Helen Potter's efforts to come to terms with sexual abuse from her father. Helen and her pet rat run away from home and into the English countryside before confronting him face-to-face. It is recommended for middle and high school students.

A Treasury of Victorian Murder (Rick Geary, 1987–present, Nantier Beall Minoustchine).

> The books in this series combine mystery and history by exploring the life and death of figures such as Abe Lincoln, Jack the Ripper, Mary Rogers, Madeline Smith, and more. It is recommended for middle and high school students.

Truth: Red, White & Black (Robert Morales, 2004, Marvel).

> A retelling of the Captain America mythos, this book pulls from early to mid-twentieth century-history, especially that of African Americans. Steve Rogers, the blonde-haired patriot transformed into Captain America, is on a quest to learn the truth behind the experiments that lead to his status. In a nod to the Tuskegee experiments, it is revealed that African American soldiers were the guinea pigs and the only remaining survivor is actually the original Captain America. This book makes an excellent pairing with Ellison's *Invisible Man*. It is recommended for high school students.

Understanding Comics: The Invisible Art (Scott McCloud, 1994, HarperPerennial).

> Basically a course in how to read and understand comics, this text, presented in the comic book form, is excellent for introducing teachers and students to the complexity of sequential art narratives and their rich and diverse history. Once they explore this text, students will understand how to give any comic strip, comic book, or graphic novel a deeper reading for both form and content. It is recommended for high school students.

Watchmen (Alan Moore and Dave Gibbons, 1987, DC Comics).

> The comic book series that revolutionized the superhero, this complex text examines the popular culture and geopolitics of the 1980s, as various former superheroes try to find their way in a world that may or may not need them. The *Moby-Dick* of graphic novels, it can be studied on various levels of intricacy and its nuances never seem to be exhausted. It is recommended for mature high school students.

X-Men: Dark Phoenix Saga (Chris Claremont and John Byrne, 2006, Marvel).

> The quintessential X-Men story, this saga spans galaxies, as Jean Grey struggles to control the cosmic and destructive Phoenix force within her. A story of sacrifice and existential choices, the tale galvanized the characterization and motivation of the remaining X-Men stories for a generation. It is recommended for middle and high school students.

Editor

James Bucky Carter is a PhD student in English education at the University of Virginia. He has taught middle and high school in North Carolina, as well as first-year composition and literature classes at the community college and university level, and recently taught the Literature for Adolescents class at the University of Virginia. His work has appeared in *The International Journal of Comic Art, ImageTexT, Marvels and Tales, The Encyclopedia of African American Literature*, and *The Art of College Teaching: 28 Takes*. He is a lifelong reader of sequential art narratives and has incorporated them into his curriculum at every level of teaching. Currently, he is a visiting instructor in English education at the University of Southern Mississippi.

Contributors

Randall Clark is assistant professor of communication and media studies at Clayton State University in Atlanta, Georgia. His PhD is from Bowling Green State University, and he has been teaching communications courses since 1989. He finds comic books and graphic novels to be invaluable teaching tools, used as a means of introducing students to archetypal characters and semiotic structure and analysis. He has also been a serious comic book collector for four decades, with particular interest in the silver age. His publications include a book on exploitation movies and a study of the children's book series *Freddy the Pig*.

Douglas Fisher and Nancy Frey are on the faculties of Hoover High School and San Diego State University. They teach English to high school students, as well as methods courses to university students as part of the City Heights Educational Collaborative Professional Development School. Their article "Using Graphic Novels, Anime, and the Internet in an Urban High School," published in *English Journal*, won the Farmer Award for Outstanding Writing from the National Council of Teachers of English.

Brandon Guisgand was a student of Allen Webb's at Western Michigan University when he collaborated with his professor to write their essay for this collection.

Marla Harris is an independent scholar with a PhD from Brandeis University. She has taught writing and literature courses at the University of Tennessee and the University of Minnesota and currently conducts creative writing classes and book discussion groups for middle and high school students. Her essays have appeared in *African American Review, Children's Literature in Education, Children's Literature Association Quarterly,* and *The Lion and the Unicorn*. She grew up reading Archie and Superman comics, and now she and her students often share graphic novels in their discussions. She first read *Persepolis* at the urging of an Iranian friend.

Don Leibold has been an English language arts teacher for more than eleven years. He has taught in middle and high school and in alternative schools in Milwaukee, Wisconsin, and Houston, Texas. In the spring of 1999, his fellow teachers at Deady Middle School in Houston named him Teacher of the Year. He has had articles published in *Classroom Notes Plus, Signal,* and *Voices from the Middle* and poetry published in the *Milwaukee Journal Sentinel*. He has been reading X-Men comic books for nearly thirty years.

J. D. Schraffenberger is a PhD student in English at Binghamton University in New York, where he teaches courses in creative writing, composition, and literature. His work has appeared or is forthcoming in *English Journal, The Journal of Kentucky Studies, The Louisville Review, The Seattle Review, The Paterson Literary Review, Syntax,* and elsewhere. Inspired early on by the work of the late John Gardner (*Grendel*), he has been seeking an outlet for his passion for *Beowulf* and wrote this essay because he recently explored using Hinds's graphic novel with his own students, who had previously found the epic poem boring.

Allen Webb is a former high school teacher of English and mass media and currently professor of English, English education, and postcolonial studies at Western Michigan University. Author of three books, including *Literature and Lives: A Response-Based, Cultural Studies Approach to Teaching English* (2001), and more than twenty-five articles, he is committed to social justice teaching and is currently investigating the potential of new technologies and multimodal approaches to learning.

Stephen Weiner is director of the Maynard Public Library in Massachusetts and holds an MA in children's literature as well as an MLIS. He has been writing about comic art since 1992. His articles and reviews have appeared in *Voice of Youth Advocates, Library Journal, School Library Journal, English Journal, Bookmarks,* and other publications. His books include *Bring an Author to Your Library* (1993), *100 Graphic Novels for Public Libraries* (1996), *The 101 Best Graphic Novels* (2001), *Faster Than a Speeding Bullet: The Rise of the Graphic Novel* (2003), and *The 101 Best Graphic Novels: Revised Edition* (2005). In addition, he is coauthor (with N. C. Christopher Couch) of *The Will Eisner Companion* (2004).

This book was typeset in Palatino and Helvetica by Electronic Imaging.
Typefaces used on the cover include Anatasia and Nueva.
The book was printed on 50-lb. Accent Opaque paper by Versa Press, Inc.